"*Thinking, Listening, Being* is a well-writte[n] [disci]plines in the Wesleyan tradition. Firmly r[ooted in Scripture] tive, and practically defined, these disciplines are essential t[o Christian ministry.] Every pastor will benefit from this excellent work."

—Dr. Jesse C. Middendorf
General Superintendent Emeritus
Church of the Nazarene

"Taking seriously the expectations of a 'cruciform life' that flow from a pastoral call, Jeren Rowell has presented an accessible yet convicting resource for pastors of all traditions. . . . He steps into our lives as an ecclesial guide, fellow churchmen, and trusted pastor, reminding us all that we are to be resident theologians in the beautiful places God has called us."

—Dr. John Megyesi
Pastor
Lowell, Massachusetts, First Church of the Nazarene

"In a day and age when leaders are inundated with resources, Rowell brings into sharp focus the unique aspects of Wesleyan pastoral leadership. His transparent model of authentic leadership is more than necessary in our world today. . . . a vital resource, [this book] reminds pastors of the essentials in ministry, providing a firm theological foundation on which to build the practical aspects of ministry."

—Dr. Carla Sunberg
President
Nazarene Theological Seminary

"Finally, we have a book written by someone who understands deeply the practice of the pastoral office. Dr. Jeren Rowell has not given us some suggested practices that might work if we try real hard. He has offered us the most comprehensive vision for the contemporary pastor to date. The words on these pages are indicative of a man who has given his life to modeling pastoral integrity for us and mentoring those of us who desire to embrace the heart of God in ministry."

—Rev. Phil Hamner
Pastor
Overland Park, Kansas, Church of the Nazarene

"Jeren Rowell's *Thinking, Listening, Being* is an extraordinary book written from a pastor's heart. Be careful: this book will feed your spirit! [Rowell reminds] pastors distracted by strategies and statistics . . . that God's metric is very different. [And he introduces] fatigued, heartbroken, and disappointed pastors . . . to Jesus again."

—Rev. Jeff Barker
Associate Professor of Practical Theology
Eastern Nazarene College

"This book was a breath of fresh air in my soul! I wish every pastor—whether he or she is a veteran or a rookie, pastoring a large church or a small one, riding a wave of good tidings or stuck in the muck of church messiness—would read this book. In its pages the pastor would find help, hope, and the encouragement to move forward in Christ!"

—Rev. Rob Prince
Pastor
Flint, Michigan, Central Church of the Nazarene

"In the opening sentence of the introduction Rowell asks, 'Do we really need another book about pastoral theology and practice?' I would like to answer by saying that we do need another book like this one. This book is firmly anchored in the biblical and theological understandings of the church that are so foundational to effective service in ministry today. In this day of instant messaging and brief sound bites, Rowell challenges the reader to examine and reflect deeply on the implications of God's call to ministry as the job description unfolds throughout the Scriptures."

—Dr. Bruce Petersen
Professor of Pastoral Ministry
Mount Vernon Nazarene University

"Jeren Rowell's *Thinking, Listening, Being: A Wesleyan Pastoral Theology* comes from a profound love, devotion, and care for the pastoral office as an overflow of his love of the church and ultimately God. On the surface and in the deep marrow of this work is a conviction that such a sacred calling to the pastoral office is actually not about the pastor but about opening oneself to being used as God's servant as a prophetic shepherd of God's flock. Rowell reminds us that pastors are not called to a consumeristic helping profession but to a vocation of prophetic servanthood."

—Dr. Brent Peterson
Associate Professor of Theology
Northwest Nazarene University

"*Thinking, Listening, Being: A Wesleyan Pastoral Theology* is a great addition to any collection of practical theology. Specifically, the writing of Jeren Rowell assists all those in ministry to explore the vocational life of the pastor in rich, thoughtful, and meaningful ways. His depth of research and real-life experience shines through the pages. I found myself nodding my head in agreement through much, pausing to consider a piece of new wisdom with thankfulness, and occasionally saying 'ouch' along the way. I believe each amen, pause, and 'ouch' was good for my soul."

—Dr. Mary Rearick Paul
Vice President for Spiritual Development
Point Loma Nazarene University

THINKING | LISTENING | BEING
A WESLEYAN PASTORAL THEOLOGY

JEREN ROWELL

BEACON HILL PRESS
OF KANSAS CITY

Beacon Hill Press of Kansas City
PO Box 419527
Kansas City, MO 64141
BeaconHillBooks.com

ISBN 978-0-8341-3246-7

Printed in the
United States of America

Cover Design: Ryan Deo
Interior Design: Sharon Page

The Internet addresses, email addresses, and phone numbers in this book are accurate at the time of publication. They are provided as a resource. Beacon Hill Press of Kansas City does not endorse them or vouch for their content or permanence.

Library of Congress Cataloging-in-Publication Data
Rowell, Jeren, 1961-
  Thinking, listening, being : a Wesleyan pastoral theology / Jeren Rowell.
    pages cm
  Includes bibliographical references.
  ISBN 978-0-8341-3246-7 (pbk.)
  1. Pastoral theology—Wesleyan Church. 2. Wesleyan Church—Doctrines. I. Title.
  BV4011.3.R69 2014
  253—dc23
                                                      2014006170

10 9 8 7 6 5 4 3 2 1

Let it not be imputed to forwardness, vanity, or presumption, that one who is of little esteem in the Church takes upon him thus to address a body of people, to many of whom he owes the highest reverence.
—John Wesley, An Address to the Clergy (February 6, 1756)

To the great company of co-vocational pastors.
I honor your embrace of assignments that require your tentmaking lifestyle. As your tribe increases, may you always be a thoughtful and purposeful corps of good and godly pastors.

CONTENTS

FOREWORD

Practical divinity was a favorite phrase used by John Wesley to describe how theology educates, equips, and sustains pastors to shepherd God's flock. He understood not only that a pastor is the theologian-in-residence for a congregation but also that everything a pastor does is an expression of what that pastor believes about God and the church. Practical divinity is the appropriate balance between right belief (orthodoxy) and right practice (orthopraxy). When beliefs are lived out in inconsistent ways, they are not credible. When practices are not tethered to foundational beliefs, they are misguided. That's why what a pastor believes and what a pastor does cannot be separated. Orthodoxy and orthopraxy go together. This is the Wesleyan way of ministry.

The apostle Paul emphasized practical divinity when he charged his young mentee, Timothy,

> Devote yourself to the public reading of Scripture, to preaching and to teaching. Do not neglect your gift, which was given you through prophecy when the body of elders laid their hands on you. Be diligent in these matters; give yourself wholly to them, so that everyone may see your progress. Watch your life and doctrine closely. Persevere in them, because if you do, you will save both yourself and your hearers. (1 Tim. 4:13-16)

Good advice for any young pastor.

This is also ordination language. Every time I read Paul's words, I remember the night that my wife and I knelt at the altar of College

Church of the Nazarene, and General Superintendent John A. Knight laid his hands on my head and said: "I charge thee before God and the Lord Jesus Christ:

Preach the Word;

Watch thou in all things;

Endure afflictions;

Do the work of an evangelist;

Make full proof of thy ministry.

Take thou authority to administer the sacraments, and to take oversight of the Church of God."

Though these ordination vows were spoken more than twenty years ago, they are still instructive to me. To "make full proof of my ministry" simply means that by the grace of God I will endeavor to fulfill everything God has called and prepared me to do. I will preach God's Word faithfully. I will endure hardship joyfully. I will proclaim the gospel generously. I will administer the holy sacraments humbly. I will lead the church wisely. And I will do all of these things keeping a careful watch over my life and my words so that in the doing of these things, I exalt the risen Christ and not myself. This is the Wesleyan way of ministry.

I was a young seminarian when I first met Jeren Rowell. I had been blessed with exceptional pastoral mentors in my life, but up until that point I had never worked as closely with someone who took practical divinity so seriously. Working side by side with Jeren reinforced my conviction that how a pastor was formed theologically really mattered in the day-to-day things a pastor did. His example taught me that being theologically minded and practically oriented was not a contradiction. He demonstrated systems and structures for ministry that were not based on passing fads or current trends but could withstand the test of time. They would be the kind of bedrock pastoral practices that could keep me steady and provide endurance over the long haul.

Jeren has been one of my closest friends for more than two decades. I have seen him in a variety of different situations, circumstances, and settings. I can think of no one more qualified to write a book about pastoral theology and practice than Jeren Rowell. He has served as an associate pastor in two churches and as senior pastor of the same congregation for fourteen years, and he now serves as the superintendent of a growing district of nearly one hundred churches. In *Thinking, Listening, Being,* Jeren has done more than describe a practical divinity—he shows us how to live it.

—David A. Busic
General Superintendent, Church of the Nazarene
Season after Pentecost 2013

PREFACE

How is it that one comes to love something? I love baseball, but I am not entirely sure why I do. Especially as a nearly thirty-year fan of the Chicago Cubs, I ask myself every September why I endure this annual hardship. But my love for baseball isn't really about any particular team, player, or place. It is really about a way of being that has more to do with the nearly indescribable nuances of the game that are as meaningful around a hot stove in December as they are sitting along the third-base line in July. These are the kinds of things that casual observers of the game do not recognize and may not understand even if they were pointed out. More visceral than strategy or statistics, these heart-deep connections to the game are what can cause an otherwise rational person to pull the car over and spontaneously watch a couple of innings played by neighborhood nine-year-olds on a do-it-yourself diamond in a vacant lot.

In a similar way, I am not sure I can describe adequately why I love being a pastor. It certainly has something to do with the theologically reflective practices that I have tried to describe in this book, but somehow even these ideas do not fully explain why a person would love this work so. Truthfully, there is much about it these days that is not very lovely. Pastoral ministry tends to take perfectly good Christians and toss them—educated, trained, and ordained—into the gristmill of congregational life. The person that emerges after forty or fifty years of pastoral work is vastly different from what we would have witnessed had the church left the person alone. Nevertheless, most pastors will testify to a love for the life and work of a pastor that defies rational analysis. No matter how difficult this work may become, we know that we have been invited into a profound grace under which we participate with God in the beautiful work of announcing good news to the world.

I have a vivid memory of when this love really began to capture my heart. In the autumn of 1979, I began my journey of educational preparation to become a pastor. The first courses I attended were part of the general liberal arts core, so I was excited to begin the first course in what was called the pre-seminary major. It was a beautiful Monday evening when I walked to Williams Hall and entered the classroom for an introductory Christian ministry class taught by Dr. A. E. Sanner.

That first class session was normal in every way until we came near the end of the evening. In a moment of special inspiration Dr. Sanner began to speak passionately—preach really—about the burdensome joy of pastoral work and of a life given to the service of Christ and the church. I have not forgotten the climactic moment of that rousing message when with tears in his eyes he looked into the hope-filled and naive faces of his students. We were so eager to "get on with it" and yet somehow, under the unction of the Spirit, he sparked in us a vision for a whole life of learning and service. He said, "Tonight, I see the stars shining in your eyes as you dream of fulfilling the call that God has placed in your hearts. Across the years I have seen far too many of those shining lights grow dim and even go out. It need not be that way. Brothers and sisters, keep them shining! Keep them shining! Keep them shining!"

As I walked back across the campus that night toward my room in Chapman Hall, I was aware that something had happened in me that remains to this very day. A vision was cast that later I would hang on the words of Charles Wesley, also first given to me by Dr. Sanner, "Let us unite the two so long disjoined: knowledge and vital piety."

Two aspects of this story gave shape to the present work. One is a focus on students, those who are just beginning the journey of responding to the call of God. Among the greatest of gifts I have received is the gift of mentors. Consistently throughout my life I have been blessed by the teaching and influence of elders in ministry who poured their knowledge and wisdom into me for no better reason than a conviction that this is what one does with gifts: pass them on. From that same conviction I am compelled to gather these reflections on the good and difficult work of pastoral ministry. I hope that they may help those following me, especially those who are just learning what it means to say yes to a life of vocational ministry. For these friends, I hope that this book may find its way into classrooms and mentoring groups to initiate and guide learning conversations.

Second is the aspect of seeking to model a particular way of going about pastoral work that unites passionate love for God's people and for the world with the disciplines of careful study and theological reflection. This uniting of knowledge and love expresses a critical point of need for the contemporary church. As others have noted, too many pastors enter the work with little more than a vague sense of wanting to help people. This only serves to weaken the very idea of *pastor*, not to mention the actual execution of the office. On the other hand, others respond to the call of God, recognize the need for careful preparation, but then find themselves in a virtual cul-de-sac of education with little connection to pastoral mission. Between these ditches is a road of faithful and effective pastoral life that is walked by countless men and women who day after day, mostly unnoticed by church hierarchy and the world, do the work of prayerfully guiding God's people on "the upward call of God in Christ Jesus" (Phil. 3:14, ESV).

—Jeren Rowell
In the twenty-eighth year of my ordination

INTRODUCTION

Do we really need another book about pastoral theology and practice? A casual search of available books on pastoral life actually does nothing to suggest that we are in danger of too many perspectives on this important role in the church, so I will attempt to add my own. My motivation for this work is really quite personal. At the heart of it is the fact that I possess, for reasons I cannot fully explain, a passionate concern for this work and its implication for the church. This was developed in me partly through twenty-five years of local parish ministry. In this regard I am indebted not only to good mentor-colleagues but also and perhaps especially to laypersons who, although they respected their pastor, did not imagine that a young pastor was beyond teaching. These mature Christians were able to express more than what they needed from their pastor, appreciated as that was by me. They particularly testified to what God was speaking to them through prayer and their own study of the Scriptures—ideas about who we should be and what we should do as a congregation trying to be faithful to the gospel and effective in mission. The past eight years of working as an overseer (*superintendent* in the language of my denomination) has only deepened my conviction that doing everything I can to help pastors do their work well is a worthy effort.

I do encounter many good pastors who not only fulfill their ministries with love and skill but also teach me and challenge me in my own thinking and practice of pastoral life. At times, however, I also encounter assigned ministers who are clearly failing the pastoral office. This incompetence is often displayed by the dysfunction of the congregations they were called to serve. There is not a clear sense of identity as the people of God, no real biblical or theological coherence to the works of the congregation, and little sense of security that should be inspired by a pastor whose faithful life reflects the presence of the Good Shepherd. The church has too often seemed willing to suffer these losses provided they do not become too pervasive—a sort of "oh well, can't win them all" attitude. We take our losses, mitigate the damage, and try to do better with the next assignment. This is unacceptable for many reasons, not the least of which is the one expressed by Andrew Purves in an ordination sermon, "God will not be mocked by faithless or incompetent pastors."[1] I agree but also recognize the heavy responsibility this places on the very church that educated, affirmed, and eventually credentialed these ministers whose lives betray their holy calling. It is not enough for the church collectively to cluck its tongue at these shameful examples and move on. We must do better in the calling, preparation, ordination, and ongoing accountability of all who would take up the offices of Christ on behalf of the people of God.

This is not to suggest that sick congregations are only explained by inadequate clergy. Sometimes congregations are dysfunctional because of their corporate disobedience and sin (more on that later). On the matter of clergy, how did we ever end up with pastors who are not "making full proof" of their ministries? Asking this question is not seeking to lay blame but to identify some areas where the church may be able to improve its ministerial preparation. On this point, it is evident to me that some pastors were simply not prepared well. The seminal responsibility for this failure falls right back on pastors themselves in the mentoring process. An essential component of pastoral work is to inspire and nurture the call of God in the lives of people whom God is drawing into pastoral vocation. Sometimes this calling is stillbirthed through the carelessness of a pastor whose own practice of ministry does nothing to cast a vision for or inspire confidence in the high and holy calling of pastoral work. All pastors should be sharply aware that they are potentially modeling vocational ministry for the people watching them (especially children) in ways that they probably do not realize at the time. Once a person testifies to an emerging sense of calling, the responsibility of the pastor intensifies.

My story in this regard is a model, not because of me, but because of the good and faithful pastor with which I was blessed when God's call began becoming clearer in my life.[2] Somewhere around my fifteenth year I began to sense the Spirit nudging me toward imagining a life of service to Christ and the church as a pastor. I had no confidence that I possessed the gifts and grace necessary to fulfill that kind of calling, but I began to entertain the idea that perhaps through my gifts of music I could offer something of value to a congregation.

Along the way, through conversations with my parents and eventually with my pastor, I was willing to begin testifying that I believed God was calling me to preach from a life wholly given over to pastoral ministry. What happened next is what I dream of every pastor doing who becomes aware of this call in the life of a parishioner. My pastor could easily have said, "Well, son, that's just fine. Now off to college and seminary with you and they will get you ready." Pastor Wallace did, in fact, help me get to college, but he did something else that was critical to good preparation. He immediately wrapped me into his vocational life. He and his wife took me inside the life and work of a pastor. He regularly invited me into his study, showing me his books and how he used them to study for sermons and how he prepared to preach each Sunday. He took me with him to visit in the homes of congregants and at the hospital bedside of dying saints. More than once I stood at his elbow while he held their hands, sang hymns, read Scripture, and prayed the Lord's mercy over them. Can you imagine how a young man's idea of pastoral life was profoundly shaped by these experiences? But more than these pastoral actions, it was the character of the man and the prayerful conversations about the joy of having been called to this work that ignited in me a positive and robust view of what it means to be a pastor.

The particulars would be different in other contexts and times, but this kind of mentoring is needed more than ever in the church. My expectation as a superintendent is that every pastor under my oversight purposefully raises up and develops future pastoral leaders.

A critical component of preparation that can be short-circuited is formal education. One practical and contemporary reason for this is the skyrocketing cost of education. Less than thirty years ago, students could make their way through college and seminary without huge financial debt. A willingness to work hard and live frugally could enable even a young family to thrive reasonably well while the pastor was being educationally prepared. Today it is not uncommon for seminary students to emerge from their educational journey with so much financial debt that the compensation of first ministry assignments will not enable them to repay the loans. My denomination began little more than a hundred years ago with a high commitment to Christian higher education and soon developed a theological seminary from the core conviction that an educated clergy is essential to our mission. Even during days of global economic pressure, the church that claims to believe in the necessity of an educated clergy must demonstrate that conviction by committing the necessary resources to solve this problem. Clearly, new ways of delivering theological education are emerging, but careful attention to substance and quality should provide critical correctives to the popular values of growth and profitability.

Perhaps more concerning than costs are the beliefs and attitudes held by some in the Wesleyan-holiness tradition that formal education for pastors is not really that important or even that it is dangerous. My work with local congregations in pastoral search reveals that while some churches clearly prefer a seminary graduate to become a candidate, other congregations are suspicious of the well-educated candidate. I do not think this is because the laypeople want their pastors to be unprepared in theology, Bible, and practical theology but because too often a rookie pastor has been unwise in applying education to ministry in a particular context. The solution is not to reduce expectations for theological education but to continue improving the strategies of educational providers that are designed to help pastors integrate and contextualize their education. The important ministry of good mentors again comes into view here. It is critical that veteran pastors and schools partner together to shape pastors who will know how to combine sound theological education with practical relational skills from which healthy pastoral ministries may emerge.

These factors seem key to understanding why some pastors fail to thrive. There are other important factors as well that must be noted and will be addressed later in this book. One of them is that some pastors are just plain lazy. In many parish settings accountability for time usage and productivity are minimal. As long as pastors show up on Sunday with something decent to say, they can probably get by for some time without a disciplined and diligent approach to ministry. I am convinced that many pastors waste many hours a week in the vacuous space of the Internet and the constant pull of social media. These can certainly be good and useful tools, but pastors must be honest with how they use them and become disciplined in their time management. These observations also relate to a concern increasingly corroborated by research, that pastors are not much different from anyone else when it comes to viewing sexually explicit material. In this area a pastor can very often fly under the radar of the church's scrutiny, but sometimes this behavior becomes painfully evident through the heartaches of a broken marriage, a shattered family, and a grieved congregation. Perhaps more debilitating than the occasional outing of an addicted pastor is the pervasive drain of spiritual power that happens when those who should be first to the pure well of spiritual formation are in fact polluting the well by their own compromise with the world. This work demands a depth of character that can bear the weight of an uncloistered life. Ministry in the messiness of real life requires prayerful attention to guarding one's heart and mind. This includes the challenge of receiving the confessions of a people who are "harassed and helpless" by a world hell-bent on their destruction. When those confessions come (and they do), only the pastor living by grace with a clear conscience and pure heart can endure. Does all of this mean that a pastor must be flawless? Of course not, but there is without doubt a pressing need among God's people these days for spiritual leaders who are models of holiness and who themselves are not in congress with the values of this world.

While there are many practical components to be discussed in each of these concerns, the key to understanding why some pastors fail to carry the office with integrity and skill is found in what others have noted well: such pastors operate on the basis of a poorly constructed pastoral theology. It is the problem of taking direction from sources other than the Scriptures and the ancient church. Recently (thinking of the past fifty years or so) the execution of the pastoral office has been so utterly captivated by the values of business leadership that a serious recovery of biblical pastoral theology is needed. This is certainly not to suggest that business leadership has nothing to offer to pastoral work, but this framework alone cannot bear the weight of spiritual leadership. Gladly, this recovery of biblical and theological foundations for pastoral leadership seems to be underway. This is the point at which I have been personally appreciative of the prolific work of Eugene H. Peterson and William Willimon, both of whom have so influenced my life that echoes of their work can no doubt be heard in me. I would also acknowledge with much gratitude and some concern the contribution of an emerging generation of pastoral leaders who dare to name what is broken about the church. The gratitude is for showing us that we must be willing to tell the truth about ourselves if we hope to grow; their holy dissatisfaction forces us to face ourselves in new ways. The concern comes when these God-called servants begin to move away from the church in bitterness or apathy rather than toward her with loving correction. Courage is needed across generations. Young leaders need the courage to risk being labeled conformists as they work to bring change and seek to learn what should be learned by those who have gone before them. This is wisdom. Older leaders need courage to repent from using the structures of power for self-protection and courage to invite and engage those who, like the men of Issachar, understand the times and know what needs to be done.[3] This is leadership.

From these concerns and convictions, I set out to gather in some kind of systematic way a theological and practical framework for thinking about, preparing for, and executing the life and work of pastor. I do not imagine that I am adding greatly to the body of work already done by people like Thomas Oden, Andrew Purves, Gordon Lathrop, Eugene Peterson, William Willimon, and others, but I offer this collection of observations with the hope that it may gain a hearing and prove helpful in some way to my relatively small tribe of Wesleyan-holiness pastors.

The scope of this work is not intended to be entirely academic nor entirely practical, but theological reflections on the life and work of a pastor. This is not only a framework from which to do this work but also a pedagogy of sorts in that this is the very nature of pastoral life, particularly in the Wesleyan tradition. Good pastoral work is always a union of orthodoxy (right belief) and orthopraxy (right practice), and this union is ever dynamic. This means the pastor must daily be about the work of theological reflection in the midst of the practical execution of ministry.

Gordon Lathrop imagines the pastor as a symbol among symbols, which means, in part, that pastors model "lifelong relearning" as they seek always to bring Scripture and the life of the church into vibrant and shaping dialogue.[4] This was essential to John Wesley's work and is a major part of the sense in which I offer this simple project as Wesleyan pastoral theology and practice. Howard Snyder notes that Wesley was "constantly engaged in the *practice* of mission . . . and *constantly reflecting theologically* on what he was doing."[5]

During my recent sabbatical I was challenged by two prominent bishops to remember that pastors who are working as overseers must never allow their work to become overshadowed by the relentless press of administrative detail. Rather, we must give first attention to prayer, study of the Scriptures, and theological reflection that is shared through spiritual direction. Working in this way could not only be a gift of love for the church but also an important model for parish pastors who also are tempted to surrender first things to the urgencies and temptations of contemporary life. I have recommitted my life to these first works and challenge my colleagues who are overseers to do the same. From this commitment I now offer the present work first to the glory of God and, as God wills, to the edification of the church.

Part 1

GOOD THINKING:
WESLEYAN PASTORAL THEOLOGY

1
THINKING WESLEYAN

To think Wesleyan is to begin with Scripture. John Wesley famously attested to being a man of one book.[1] What he meant by this was clearly a testimony to his conviction about the primacy of canonical Scripture, yet he also recognized other resources in the work of interpreting Scripture and for thinking theologically about the work to which God called him. Wesley's understanding is well known, that while Scripture is foundational and that we should "enjoin nothing that the Bible does not enjoin,"[2] still the church receives Scripture through complementary resources like tradition, reason, and experience.[3]

Tradition in this conversation is understood as the church's interpretation of Scripture, particularly the writings of ancient Christian leaders, such as Clement of Rome, Ignatius, and Polycarp. Wesley thought these apostolic fathers to be the most reliable teachers of Scripture mainly because of their proximity to the Christ event—being "nearest the fountain," as he put it. By *reason* is understood the grace-enabled ability to apply learning and logic to the interpretation of Scripture. Wesley's life and writing demonstrate his own deep appreciation for knowledge through science and argument.[4] However, the idea of reason here is more than rational ability. Reason is connected deeply to experience because the ideas from Scripture represent our relationship with God, who reveals himself to us in the Word (the incarnate Son). *Experience* as a resource for the interpretation of Scripture has in view the personal experience believers have from knowing Christ and from being assured of a right relationship to God in Christ through the witness of the Spirit. These gifts are not private but come to us through the life of the church, gathered by the Spirit and nourished by Word and Table. Key to experience as a resource for knowing is also testimony, as God's people bear witness to the assurance, by the witness of the Spirit, of salvation and to the confirmation of sanctifying grace in their lives.

These resources work together to inform our reading of Scripture, enabling us by the help of the Holy Spirit to arrive with confidence at the knowledge of what is necessary for our salvation. This idea of the Bible's clarity "in all necessary points" is from Wesley[5] and also finds contemporary expression in my denomination's Articles of Faith, which affirm the "plenary inspiration" of Scripture and that the Bible reveals God's will to us "in all things necessary to our salvation."[6] The emphasis here is not on casting doubt on the authority of Scripture but simply on recognizing that it does not derive from a perceived ability to read and understand the separate components of Scripture literalistically. Rather, we read the Bible as a whole, affirming that it faithfully points to the story of God's redeeming movement toward humanity, culminating in the life, death, and resurrection of Jesus Christ. The authority of Scripture is the authority of God, made known to us through the testimony of Scripture, in which everything points to the authority of the universal reign of God in Christ.[7]

Biblical Pastoral Theology

From this foundation, then, I will proceed with the conviction that a Wesleyan way of reading the Bible is a faithful way to read the Bible.[8] By stating this perspective at the outset I do not intend to preclude dialogue with Christians who believe differently but to clarify my commitment to the theological framework from which I am working. A Wesleyan reading of Scripture yields a particular kind of pastoral theology. Preeminently, it must be a pastoral theology that is deeply rooted in the Scriptures themselves[9]; however, drawing a pastoral theology from the Bible must begin more broadly and deeply than simply selecting texts that appear to speak directly to the pastoral office. For example, the Pastoral Epistles (1 and 2 Timothy, Titus, perhaps Philemon) do compose a rich resource for shaping the character and conduct of pastors. The admonitions of these texts are largely about the character and integrity of a pastor, moving directly to a pastor's core activities, which are to pray, study the Scriptures, and teach. (See the excursus at the end of this chapter for a summary of these admonitions.) But developing a biblical pastoral theology must in no way be limited to a particular biblical genre. The whole of Scripture, the overarching narrative of God's redeeming work, provides the framework for beginning to understand the ministry of pastors.

Eugene Peterson demonstrates this broad biblical basis for pastoral theology in his book *Five Smooth Stones for Pastoral Work*.[10] Here he draws from the Old Testament texts of Song of Songs, Ruth, Lamentations, Ecclesiastes, and Esther—known together as the Megilloth. Peterson's project is to draw the pastoral imagination back from a contemporary reliance on psychology and leadership foci to the seminal texts of Israel's annual acts of worship (Passover, Pentecost, Ninth of Ab, Tabernacles, and Purim). The acts of worship connected with these festivals (and a fast) served to *re-member* the people of God and reorient them to their identity in ways that could, at least potentially, bring life, health, and peace. Similarly, central to faithful pastoral work is resisting the temptations of spectacle or the latest technologies (using the term in the broadest sense) and preferring the work of calling out a biblical community of faith. Doing this requires a firm grip on the ancient texts that help the contemporary church navigate the emerging realities of a post-Christendom world as a people who know that God is always at work, no matter the condition of things. God is working to redeem the world and to gather his people back into a covenant of love.

Thinking of other texts, I am drawn to the pastoral theology that is embedded in Paul's passionate writing to the Corinthian church, particularly in 2 Corinthians. Here we find not only the work of a pastoral leader but also glimpses into the motivational heart of the pastor. For example, we hear Paul say to the community, "We have conducted ourselves in . . . integrity ['holiness' (margin)] and godly sincerity" (1:12); "we have spoken freely . . . and opened wide our hearts to you" (6:11); and "I will very gladly spend for you everything I have and expend myself as well" (12:15). Many other texts can also help shape a strong pastoral imagination that reaches far beyond the use of simple technologies to the very soul of what God calls pastors to be and then to do. Examples of these texts could include Exodus, Deuteronomy, Ezekiel, Nehemiah, Jeremiah, Acts, Romans, Ephesians, and many others. Obviously, the Gospels and particularly the life and ministry of Jesus are essential components of a biblical pastoral theology, but more on those texts later. The point here is that a balanced and healthy pastoral theology is rooted in the whole story of God in Christ as divinely inspired and communicated to us in the Bible.

Historical Reflections on Pastoral Theology

Wesleyan pastoral theology also relies heavily on the classical, historical reflections of the church, or the writings of the church fathers. Many of these works are important for informing pastoral theology, but the work of Gregory the Great may represent the watershed for this area of practical theology when it was given to the church in 590. The continued availability and accessibility of *The Book of Pastoral Rule* (commonly known as *Pastoral Care*) provides an important resource for contemporary pastors who wish to add the wisdom of the church to the careful shaping of a pastoral theology. More broadly, Thomas Oden's *Classical Pastoral Care* brings together in a systematic way the reflections of the first eighteen centuries of the church, with particular attention to the patristics.[11] A very fine introduction and summary of key historical works is Andrew Purves' *Pastoral Theology in the Classical Tradition*.[12]

Distinctives in Wesleyan Pastoral Theology

This foundational location in the Bible and in church history enables Wesleyan theology to achieve one of its most important contributions: the ability to avoid the undisciplined comfort of extremes but instead to strike a via media (middle way) by navigating between the dialectical tensions that are part of doing theology. An important component of this is the embrace of Wesley's idea of a "catholic spirit," meaning in part a humble willingness to recognize that one's view of things should be open for debate and possibly for correction.

A Christian may hold firm views but should also live in sincere fellowship with Christians who hold differing opinions. This is certainly not to suggest a watering down of the gospel or a lack of passionate conviction about essential matters. However, the ability to engage in charitable conversations about potentially divisive subjects should be a mark of any pastor who would bear the character of a Wesleyan pastoral theology. An open mind, warm heart, and gentle spirit are more than personality traits. They are critical strategies for engaging people and cultures that seem to be quickly gravitating toward suspicion and division. This kind of spirit should help to inspire in pastors the patience and mercy needed when working with people who are truly free to respond to the prevenient grace of God.

Additionally, a Wesleyan way of reading Scripture nurtures a distinct pastoral theology significantly because it locates pastoral identity as a particular kind of participation in the story of God, rather than in certain structures or models. One way this works out is through the conviction that the essential work of a pastor is to keep the community of faith focused on God and on what God is doing in the world. However, the ways in which the life and work of pastors has been understood lately seem to move more toward organizational leadership with its attendant measures of success than toward the prophetic work of calling out a people to live as an expression of the in-breaking kingdom of God in the world. These foci do not necessarily need to be mutually exclusive, since leadership is indeed an important component of pastoral work, but there is an order and priority to these things that enables the leadership practices of a pastor to serve the larger vision of announcing the universal reign of God in Christ.

All of this is centered in the affirmation of God as triune. Although this affirmation is obviously not uniquely Wesleyan, it is especially important in Wesleyan theology because the overarching ethos of how life in the church is conceived is the ethos of love. This is rooted in the *perichoretic* love of the Trinity. *Perichoresis* is a word used early in the church (Gregory of Nazianzus) to speak of the intimate oneness of Father, Son, and Spirit—the holy community of persons out of which flows the holy community of God's people, gathered by the Spirit as the body of Christ, the church. As pastors live and serve as representatives of Christ, this image begins to shape an understanding of pastor as lover—not in any sentimental way—but in an essential way as persons called out from and then back into the church to live and serve first and foremost from the grace of self-sacrificing love. This way of pastoring has many implications but none more basic than the simple idea of a pastor imitating the ministry of Jesus. A robust Christology is critical, not only because of what atonement means and its implications for pastoral work but also because of the importance of perceiving in the life of Jesus of Nazareth the seminal model for pastoral work. Entire books are written on this point alone, but here I would mention three essential movements in the life and ministry of Jesus that give definition to the core traits of good pastors.

The Pastoral Example of Jesus

First among these is the complete relational nature of ministry. Jesus began by gathering disciples with the simple call "Follow me." This movement of going everywhere with Jesus is not only in accord with the realities of rabbinic practices in the first century but also organic. That is to say, the essence of pastoring after the pattern of Jesus is intimate engagement with people in the basic structures of life. It is walking with them, eating with them, listening, teaching, correcting, comforting, sending, and more. It is loving people far beyond the sentimentalities of a superficial social exchange; it is loving them as deeply as parents love their children. In fact, pastoring is much like parenting in the way the covenant love of the parent-child relationship utterly rearranges and reprioritizes the life of the parent to the point that every parent knows his or her life is no longer his or her own and never again will be.

A second movement for ministry patterned after Jesus is the constant rhythm of action and contemplation. The flow of gospel narratives is back and forth from the actions of ministry (teaching, healing, comforting) to moments of reflection through prayer and conversation. This kind of rhythm is critical for the emergence of a healthy pastoral ministry. The relentless demands of people who are needy combined with the weight of carrying spiritual authority and responsibility for a people would be crushing if not for the God-given gifts of rest, reflection, and renewal. The overall structure of this book begins with thinking because so often pastoral work defaults to acting. There are so many things to be done, so many demands to meet and expectations to manage, that protecting space to think (pray and reflect) is a critical pastoral discipline, one that was modeled by our Lord.

Third, there is a sacramental movement to the ministry of Jesus. By this I mean to reflect not so much on the sacraments proper (although these are at the core) but especially on the life-giving relational exchange of call and response. That is, the call of the gospel that is announced by the church and particularly by pastoral ministry calls people to faith responses that are and which become means of grace for the church and for the world. I am talking about the whole life of the church in a way that calls us from the compartmentalizing or fracturing of Christian life. The call is toward a holistic, unified way of living together as the people of God, gathered and also sent by the Spirit, under the guidance of godly pastors. When this kind of grace-filled rhythm characterizes the community of faith, then it becomes a means of grace, a sacramental life enacted especially when the church comes to the Communion table. Keeping this identity in sharp focus can only happen when God's people fix their collective gaze on Jesus, "the pioneer and perfecter of faith" (Heb. 12:2), and this is the central work of pastors.

These ways of thinking about pastoral ministry are biblical ways of thinking. They are also in constant motion from the Scriptures, through prayer, into the life of the church and world, and then back to prayer as the church (particularly the pastor) reflects on what God is doing and what it means to join God in these works.

EXCURSUS
Biblical Cues for Pastoral Theology

2 Corinthians

1:4   "we can comfort those in any trouble with the comfort we ourselves receive from God"

1:12   "we have conducted ourselves . . . with integrity"

1:13   "we do not write you anything you cannot read or understand"

2:4   "I wrote you out of great distress and anguish of heart and with many tears"

2:17   "we do not peddle the word of God for profit"

• 3:5   "our competence comes from God"

3:12   "we are very bold"

4:2   "we do not use deception, nor do we distort the word of God"

4:5   "what we preach is not ourselves, but Jesus Christ as Lord"

4:10   "we always carry around in our body the death of Jesus"

4:16   "we do not lose heart"

• 4:18   "we fix our eyes not on what is seen, but on what is unseen"

5:11   "since . . . we know what it is to fear the Lord, we try to persuade others"

5:16   "we regard no one from a worldly point of view"

• 5:20   "we are therefore Christ's ambassadors"

6:3   we put no stumbling block in anyone's path

6:11   "we have spoken freely . . . and opened wide our hearts to you"

10:3   "we do not wage war as the world does"

10:5   "we take captive every thought to make it obedient to Christ"

11:28   "I face daily the pressure of my concern for all the churches"

12:10   "when I am weak, then I am strong"

12:15   "I will very gladly spend for you everything I have and expend myself as well"

1 Timothy

1:3   "stay there"

4:7   "train yourself to be godly"

4:12   "set an example"

- 4:13   "devote yourself to the public reading of Scripture, to preaching and to teaching"

4:15   "give yourself wholly"

4:16   "watch your life and doctrine closely"

5:1   "do not rebuke . . . but exhort"

5:3   recognize widows

5:17   honor elders

5:21   "do nothing out of favoritism"

5:22a   "do not be hasty in the laying on of hands"

5:22c   "keep yourself pure"

5:23   manage your physical health

6:10   flee from love of money

6:11   "pursue righteousness, godliness, faith, love, endurance and gentleness"

6:17   command the rich to be generous

6:20   "guard what has been entrusted to your care"

2 Timothy

1:8   "do not be ashamed of the testimony about our Lord"

1:14   "guard the good deposit that was entrusted to you"

2:1   "be strong in the grace that is in Christ Jesus"

2:3   "join with me in suffering"

2:8   "remember Jesus Christ"

2:14   warn the people of false teachers

2:15   "correctly handle the word of truth"

2:22   "flee the evil desires of youth"

2:23   "don't have anything to do with foolish and stupid arguments"

2:25   gently instruct those who oppose you; don't be resentful

3:5   have nothing to do with godless people

3:14   "continue in what you have learned and have become convinced of"

4:2   "preach the word; be prepared in season and out of season; correct, rebuke and encourage—with great patience and careful instruction"

Titus

1:13   "rebuke [false teachers] sharply"
2:1   "teach what is appropriate to sound doctrine"
2:3   "teach the older women to be reverent"
2:6   "encourage the young men to be self-controlled"
2:7   "set them an example by doing what is good"
2:9   teach submission to authority
2:15   "do not let anyone despise you"
3:10   avoid divisiveness

2
THINKING THEOLOGICALLY

Hearing a pastor say, "Well, I'm no theologian," causes me to wince more than anything else I could hear. Every pastor should recognize and embrace the idea that an essential component of pastoral calling is to be a practical theologian: one who does the practical work of ministry in theologically reflective and purposeful ways. Most pastors do their work in parish settings where they serve as the theologian in residence, as the most expert person in Bible and theology that the particular community of faith is likely to encounter. This places a massive responsibility on the pastor to do this work well and to accept the disciplines of a lifelong learner. In fairness, I assume that when pastors say something like, "I am no theologian," they mean to make the qualification that their work is not as "academic" as that done by those who have earned terminal degrees in theology. We do recognize and express deep gratitude for the ministry of those who have come under the specialized disciplines of academic study and offer their gifts to the church through research, writing, and teaching. These brothers and sisters are true and highly valued partners in the gospel of Jesus Christ.

Thinking Together

To think theologically is simply to take everything we do as pastors and as congregations back to the Scriptures and to the historic Christian faith as it has been handed down to us. Certainly, fresh contextualization is critical, but unless the new work appropriately takes into account that which has gone before, it runs the risk of innovation for its own sake. While the methods for missional engagement in the world are often undergoing adjustment, these necessary changes must submit to the scrutiny of the church insofar as the church is "rightly dividing the word of truth" (2 Tim. 2:15, KJV). This sort of accountability seems especially important for those of us from expressions of the church that rise significantly from a "believer's church" or "free church" ecclesiology. Our emphasis on the priesthood of all believers must carry with it the balancing doctrine of submission to the authority of the community of faith.

As those in the Wesleyan-holiness movement might testify, there are times for renewal and perhaps even for protest, but these times are rare and must be prayerfully surrendered to the lordship of Jesus Christ and to an ecclesiology that recognizes the authority of the church under the power of the Spirit. The point here is simply that thinking theologically is not an individual enterprise but one that takes place in communion, first in the fellowship of one's own tradition and then in the larger fellowship of the Christian church.

This can happen in several ways, including the pastoral discipline of reading well. Good pastors learn to ask questions of colleagues about what they are reading. Pastors should be of such an intellectual bearing and spiritual maturity that they are able to read widely and well beyond their own traditions.

Another important way to do theology communally is through the practice of Christian conference. This is something the Wesleys appreciated and practiced. It is engaging in prayerful conversation about doctrine and practice, not to stake out positions or win arguments, but to discern together the work of the Spirit in guiding God's church "into all the truth" (John 16:13).

Ministerial Preparation

Under this theme of thinking theologically, however, I actually have in mind more than the particular disciplines of biblical, historical, and philosophical theology. I resonate with how Wesley seemed to understand what is required for one to be an able pastor, involving a full-bodied educational preparation as well as continuing interest and learning. Wesley thought pastors should be students of logic, science, language, history, and literature, as well as the studies of Scripture and the writings of the church fathers. This does not imply that every pastor must have exhaustive knowledge of these vast areas of study, but a well-rounded general understanding and working vocabulary is a part of the kind of intellectual pursuit to which every pastor is called.

I remember well how this value for broad competency was pressed into me by an undergraduate professor who challenged the pre-seminary majors to pay attention in liberal arts courses such as music and art in the Western world and Western civilization. His reason, which seemed compelling to me, was to imagine pastoring a fourteen-year-old prodigy in classical music, for example. The professor said something like, "If that boy finds out you know nothing of Mozart or Beethoven, he will pass you off as a dummy!" I get the impression that Wesley could have said something quite similar. In fact, speaking of the various "branches of knowledge" that are part of a comprehensive education Wesley said, "What can be argued for a person who has had an University education, if he does not understand them all? Certainly, supposing him to have any capacity, to have common understanding, he is inexcusable before God and man."[1] Some may pass off this kind of expectation as a relic of Enlightenment thinking, and certainly the historical context of these comments is noted. However, in our time of narrow specialization it seems that pastors should still be people having a strong capacity for meaningful engagement with folks from many walks of life. Pastors today would be well served to broaden their interests beyond psychology, organizational leadership, and popular culture and back toward the classical bases of knowledge (language, logic, literature, science, etc.) that actually deepen one's ability to be a theologically reflective pastor. Andrew Purves writes that "competent pastors have always known about this bond, and have integrated it in such a way that the great pastors were theologians and the great theologians were pastors."[2] This by no means implies that pastors who, for legitimate reasons, did not have the benefit of formal education are somehow disqualified from ministry. This is certainly not the case, and yet it also does not remove the responsibility and challenge to be a learner, accessing every avenue and resource possible to increase one's capacity for the work.

Becoming this kind of pastor begins in the first stages of preparation. The call to preach and to serve as pastor is a call to prepare. The church understands the necessity of preparing men and women to become faithful and effective ministers of the gospel. This is why there exists a prescribed course of study for anyone pursuing ordination by the church. We might think this would be unquestioned in its value, but roadblocks seem to appear when engaging developing ministers in the disciplines of clergy preparation. One of the first barriers that may need to be overcome is the oft-expressed desire to be done with educational preparation and to "get on with it." This impulse, understandable though it may be for its passion, is dangerous when it results in ill-prepared persons accepting the sacred responsibility of spiritual leadership in a congregation. Consequently, this places significant responsibility on the church, especially as expressed in the office of overseers, to insure that ministerial preparation is done with integrity and excellence. Prior to the work of bishops, however, is the work of local pastors who usually have the first opportunity to inspire a love for learning in those whom God is calling into vocational ministry. This love for learning has to become coupled with a mind-set that the work of preparation *is* the work of ministry, not something that only precedes ministry. Once again the value of strong mentoring comes into view as an important component of this preparation.

Another potential barrier is the already mentioned prejudice (see introduction) among some against graduate or seminary education for pastors. The fear seems to be that higher learning somehow removes from students the commonsense relational skills that most laypeople think are critical to a pastor's ministry effectiveness. The responsibility to meet this prejudice is largely on the schools who must ever keep in focus that while the curriculum certainly must lay an adequate foundation for those called to further study, the key focus is on integrating (in the spirit of Charles Wesley) learning with careful contextualization and a love for God and God's people that applies the fruit of the Spirit to the power of knowing. These integrations are perhaps the most critical work of clergy preparation and simply cannot be rushed, short-circuited, or dismissed as something that just needs to be gotten out of the way.

Lifelong Learning

This conversation raises another component of thinking theologically, which is a mind-set and practice of continuous learning. This is a central idea in Wesleyan pastoral theology that rises from Wesley's own practice of constantly reflecting on the challenges of ministry and what he was doing to meet those challenges. However, not only was his a practical concern, but he made sure that his methods were rooted in Scripture.

Having the bearing and commitment of a lifelong learner is perhaps one of the most important ways to be a theologically thinking pastor. It also carries potential for some of the greatest satisfaction and joy that pastors can know. Here we are reminded that the learning is not for its own sake but is in participation with our Creator, who, by the gift of the Spirit, is always working for life, growth, and health. Lathrop notes that Martin Luther understood deeply this need to be a lifelong learner, not only of new data but especially of the rudiments of the faith. "Luther thought he had to be always beginning again, learning with the newest newcomer, the youngest child, the surprises of God's grace."[3] Temptations abound for pastors (and this could apply to any professional) to rely on knowledge and skill development that served them in the past. Certainly, experience is an irreplaceable tool for effective work, but the very competencies that enabled success in the past can quickly grow stale unless there is constant attention to "sharpen the saw," to borrow a phrase from Stephen R. Covey.[4]

The church should set specific expectations for its pastors to participate in continuing education. Nearly all professions do this as something central for a person to obtain the ongoing certification that he or she is judged worthy and well qualified to conduct the activities of the profession. Physicians, attorneys, educators, and many others understand and accept that staying abreast of research and developments in their respective fields is part of what it means to be a professional.

In the same way, pastors must embrace the call to lifelong learning, and the church must make substantive and meaningful not only the expectation for this work but also the consequence for failure to do it. I do not have in mind here punitive kinds of consequences but specific mechanisms for accountability and help. Pastors should not only be required to report on their progress in continuing education but also be challenged and assisted by collegial clergy to remedy any deficit.

Thinking theologically, while including content and the skills for using that content, is at heart really about a way of being. It is an attitude toward life and ministry that refuses to take things only at face value but always seeks to know, to understand, to see the past and look into the future, and to cast an informed vision for the life and work of God's people in the world. It is not our vision, to be sure; it is God's vision. But it does call for leaders, as it always has, to urge the people of God forward toward becoming an authentic reflection of the kingdom of God in the world.

3
THINKING IDENTITY

The ability to think precisely and wisely about pastoral work has much to do with a person's sense of identity as shaped by God and the church. Woe to the Christian who approaches pastoral ministry as little more than a career choice. True pastors are those who know they have been seized by God and have had the hands of the church laid upon them, pressing into them the sacred vows of ordained life. This is not against a person's will, however, for the surrendered will of the one who is called is an essential component of that which sets him or her apart for Christian ministry. God calls. The one called must respond with an obedient embrace of the call.

The Call of God and Church

One of the earliest lessons my first mentor gave me was the message that I should only pursue the life and work of a pastor under the firm and unwavering conviction that God was calling me to it. The repetitious advice went something like this, "Knowing that God has called you is critical because there will be many days when the only thing that holds you steady is the knowledge and conviction that God has chosen you." Thirty years in pastoral work confirmed the truth of this advice, not only in my own experience but also through the testimony of countless colleagues in ministry. It doesn't take long to realize that living and working at the intersection of grace and sin is full of danger. It is dangerous to stand as a representative of Christ before the congregation and dare to proclaim, "Thus says the Lord." It is dangerous to receive the confessions of people whose lives have been wrecked by sin. It is dangerous to be placed on a pedestal by well-meaning parishioners who easily forget that you also are a jar of clay inhabited by God's glorious treasure (2 Cor. 4:7). It is especially dangerous when pastors succumb to the temptation to become professionals, skilled in the technologies of church work but neglecting the first work of prayer. I have committed to memory of mind and heart the line in Scottish novelist George MacDonald's work *The Curate's Awakening,* where he warns, "Nothing is so deadening to the divine as a habitual dealing with the outsides of holy things."[1] When these dangers become evident, sometimes through the careless and hurtful words of the very people we seek to lead and sometimes through our own undisciplined weariness, those are the moments we rediscover our sure footing in the memory that we are here because God called us here. And by "here" I am not thinking first of geography but of vocation: the unique, fascinating, troubling, burdensome joy of pastoral life.

What does it really mean to be called? This is common conversation with those who are in the educational journey toward vocational ministry. When candidates for licensure and ordination come before the boards charged with discernment in these things, one of the key questions is about the candidate's sense of calling. "Tell us about your call to ministry," we often say. Inevitably, all who are pressed to answer such a question struggle to articulate the answer. This does not necessarily point to a lack of calling but to the challenge of holding together truthfully the passionate conviction that God is calling them with a clear articulation of how such a calling came to be. Like Samuel, we find ourselves in need of direction and assistance not only to recognize the voice of the Lord but also to learn how to put into words that which really defies language.

The temptation here may be to frame our calling in some spectacular way from the assumption that doing so would give it credibility. A few thundering voices, flashes of lightning, or angelic apparitions would bolster a person's claim that God was calling him or her into pastoral ministry. The truth is that God's calling of particular Christians into the life of service through pastoral work most often emerges over time in concert with the nurture of congregations. The work of the Spirit in calling women and men to pastoral work is neither an isolated work nor an individualistic work. The wooing of the Spirit is personal, but it is also always communal. God's call to Samuel relied significantly on the faith of Samuel's mother and on the prophet Eli to help him navigate what was happening. God's call to me came into focus largely through my community of faith and especially through my pastor, who helped me make sense of a deepening awareness of holy obligation and duty that in many ways defied what seemed the most logical choices for my life's work.

My call to ministry did not suddenly snap into focus in a moment of special inspiration. My conviction that God called me to this work developed at the convergence of a deep and inner sense of the Spirit's promptings and the recognitions of others. My family, my pastor, and my congregation saw that God was doing something in me to turn my life from the typical pursuits of an American teenager in the 1970s toward a life that would be entirely redesigned. This redesigning happened largely through the influence of a church that began to recognize and affirm God's preparatory work in me. It's not that the people had nothing to work with. To hear them tell it, there were many signs along the way that God had designs on me for the work of pastoral ministry.

As a young boy, while most boys my age were interested in imitating Johnny Unitas or Wilt Chamberlain, I was imitating our pastor leading the Sunday service, complete with songs, prayers, and sermon. The clip-on necktie clasped to my pajamas and the round piano stool wound up to its highest setting for my pulpit only added evidence to the vocation I was imagining. Even as a teenager who was most interested in music, I found myself drawn to the church building and spent many hours there in the sanctuary not only playing the piano but secretly hoping that I might catch just one additional glimpse of what the pastor actually did when most of our people were busy with other things.

I do not see these simply as cute stories of childhood. These were all signposts that a discerning community of faith wisely used to nurture the call of God in my life. It was only when my local church gave me my first local preacher's license at age seventeen that my mother revealed a story she had wisely hidden from me to that point. When I was born, my mother and my grandfather, a godly man of prayer, agreed together that the Lord was speaking to them of God's plan to use me in the service of pastoral life. I remain deeply grateful for my mother's wise restraint, for if she had told the story too soon, it could have been misread as my family calling me to be a pastor. But then I was also very thankful for the affirmation the story provided when the time was right that I was hearing correctly the nudge of the Spirit toward a life of vocational ministry.

This is why the discernment of the community is a critical component in the call and response of individuals to ordained ministry. It is not enough that a person testifies to having been called by God to serve as a pastor; the church must affirm this call on the basis of prayer, observation, and accountability over time. No matter how passionately an individual may insist on God's call, he or she should never be ordained and assigned to the awesome responsibility of a pastoral post unless the church is able to bear witness that his or her life (character and practices) demonstrates the grace and gifts for ministry.

On this point the church must also be cautioned about judging these matters according to the values of this world. God's call often seems to make no sense, and the Bible regularly provides examples of this. Samuel's mission to anoint a king took him, by the leading of God, toward the least likely and seemingly weakest candidate. We often tell the stories of Moses, Joseph, Paul, and many others who could have easily been disqualified by the world's reckoning but by grace were called, anointed, and enabled for service to God's people and to God's mission in the world.

The Basis for Identity

Taking up the life of a pastor requires a clear sense of calling not only for the reasons described above but also because this is what begins to shape a pastor's identity. Without this connection a pastor's identity could derive from particular talents and skills or from his or her unique personality. Although these features are important and useful for a pastor's self-awareness and for understanding which particular assignments he or she would best fit, pastoral identity must rest on a deeper foundation. Much has been made of understanding personality traits in recent years. Psychosocial tools (e.g., Myers-Briggs, DISC, StrengthsFinder, etc.) are indeed useful but cannot alone form the basis of pastoral identity that must come first from the knowledge of God's call and from a solid theology of the church and of the role of leaders in the church, especially overseers, pastors, and teachers. These first thoughts enable one's pastoral theology to be rooted in Scripture. It also helps the pastor resist the persistent and sometimes strong temptation to take his or her cues from the expectations of people—a dangerous and weak way to go about the work of a pastor.

This conversation also reminds us that while certain personality types may be preferred for the leadership practices valued by organizations (including religious organizations), no personality type is disqualified from grace-enabled, effective pastoral leadership. Some have argued that there is a cultural bias toward extroversion and extroverted leaders. I have had many conversations with students who knew they were being called by God and yet also knew they were introverts. They wondered if this introversion somehow sidelined them from the possibility of successful ministry. What they actually seemed to be worried about is not the ability to listen to God or to sound a prophetic call to the church and the world. Their anxiety seemed more about the culturally conditioned assumption that effective organizational leadership requires gifts that enable one to lead by force of personality in a wooing, charming, and persuading way. Confessing my own introverted bias, I actually believe that introverts can be especially gifted for pastoral ministry because their impulse is toward settings that help them attend to the core works of pastoral life, such as study and prayerful reflection. However, introverts must also learn the disciplines of taking the initiative in relationship building and engaging in conversation in order to be fully effective in people work.

47

Self-Awareness

Self-awareness is a critical task for pastors. This is why mentors are so important to our growth and development as people and as ministers. Each of us needs at least one person who is able and willing to tell us the unvarnished truth of how we come across to others. We all have quirks and blind spots that can impact our pastoral work negatively unless we are able to identify them and then, with the help of accountability partners, make the disciplined adjustments that are necessary to enjoy healthy relationships.

On this journey of healthy self-awareness, pastors should never be afraid to use the skill and insight of trained counselors and therapists. In fact, the overall health of the pastoral corps might be greatly enhanced if we could build the expectation in church culture that pastors should offer themselves to an annual health assessment. Pastors, as all Christians who are being sanctified, are not superhumanly immune to grief, anger, depression, and so forth. In one sense, a pastor's susceptibility to mental or emotional disease may be exacerbated by the sheer spiritual weight of what God has called him or her to be and to do. Again, this is dangerous work in many ways. Part of this is the reality recognized by Paul who wrote, "For our struggle is not against flesh and blood, but against the rulers, against the authorities, against the powers of this dark world and against the spiritual forces of evil in the heavenly realms" (Eph. 6:12). We need the fellowship of the ordained, the godly care of overseers, and the love of the community of faith in order to navigate safely the vulnerabilities of pastoral life.

Several years ago I experienced a spiritual, emotional, and physical crash that I now remember under the classical description of a "dark night of the soul." It came at the end of a long period when I succumbed to the temptation to do the work of ministry more from the expectations of people than from the clear sense of God's call. Consequently, I ran myself ragged. In one sense, I knew it was happening, but in my youth I had always been able to shake off the weariness and somehow find new energy to keep doing more. Not this time. There came a day when, even though I was supposed to get on another airplane and take another ministry trip, suddenly I could not even get myself out of bed. A darkness descended on me that I had never known, and it frightened me terribly.

There is a long story to be told here, but two points are especially pertinent for the present discussion. One is that although this crash was physical and emotional, it was also spiritual. That is to say, I was keenly aware of a spiritual battle with an accuser, an enemy of God and enemy of my life that I instinctively knew I could not battle on my own. Which leads to the second point: I needed help. Thanks be to God, help was nearby. My wife sprang into action by canceling schedules, building a wall of protection around me, and going to prayer for me. My district superintendent, Keith Wright, came beside me not only with his prayers and loving words but also with the needed affirmation of his continuing confidence and esteem.

I turned to my two sisters who I knew to be experienced and skilled in matters of intercessory prayer and spiritual battle. Their prayer, loving support, and wise counsel were a beautiful means of God's grace to me. My recovery, which took several days to return to normal function and several months to process fully, included significant life changes. Among these changes was the embrace of a sustainable pattern of daily physical exercise that remains to this day. This is not only about physical health but also about the management of stress that helps to keep identity in proper focus. There were other changes, including a new awareness of vulnerability that by God's grace has not become weakness but strength in the daily awareness of my need to immerse myself in Scripture, prayer, and quiet listening before the Lord.

My story may have value in practical ways, but my intention here is to connect it to this necessary component in pastoral theology of calling and identity. Thinking rightly about identity requires a solid and unrelenting grasp of how God's call totally reorders our life priorities in such a way that we simply no longer have time for many of the things that our culture, even our church culture, tells us we should know and experience. I remember Eugene Peterson saying (and perhaps writing somewhere) that for him being a pastor took a lot of time. He was not speaking of the tasks of ministry. He was speaking of time to pray, time to read, and time to think that took him away from many other possibilities offered by contemporary life.

William Willimon notes in his book *Calling and Character* that conventional wisdom suggests pastors get into trouble when they forget they are also regular people. Alternatively, Willimon suggests, "Most of the ethical problems of pastors are not due to our forgetting that we are 'persons,' but rather when we forget that we are pastors."[2] This is why thinking carefully and rightly about calling and identity is a critical pastoral discipline.

4

THINKING PRAYERFULLY

Perhaps "thinking prayerfully" is not a common way of talking. Thinking and praying may seem distinct activities, but here I have in mind something specific about what it means to think prayerfully. It is the foundation of the kind of theological reflection that I have been discussing to this point. The particular pastoral ministry of prayer will come into focus more in chapter 6 as we think about prayer as one of the core works of a pastor.

In this chapter I am attempting to give expression to something that is not really easy to talk about because it is so intuitive and spiritual. It has to do with how the Spirit shapes a mind-set (*phronousin* as in Rom. 8:5) through the manner and practices of a prayerful life that begins to form our hearing, thinking, and expression in ways that would not happen outside of this holistic, prayerful framework. Therefore, I am thinking here of prayer less in the sense of a particular spiritual discipline and more as a way of being that brings one into the reality of prayer "without ceasing" as in 1 Thessalonians 5:17. Joseph Ratzinger wrote of this well in his recent work, *Jesus of Nazareth*: "The more the depths of our souls are directed toward God, the better we will be able to pray. . . . This orientation pervasively shaping our whole consciousness, this silent presence of God at the heart of our thinking, our meditating, and our being, is what we mean by 'prayer without ceasing.'"[1]

This is the sense in which I want to talk about thinking prayerfully. It is the idea that there is a way of *being* as a pastor that moves prayer to a deeper level than does devotional discipline or pastoral intercession (though these are critical activities). It involves a sanctification wrought by the Spirit that, although entirely by grace, can only be fully known in the life of one who is utterly surrendered to God not only in the matter of relational holiness but also and especially in the matter of one's very identity. Eugene Peterson expresses it: "We need to have an existential understanding of prayer as an all-involving way of life."[2] This is not to say, as he explains, that everything a Christian does is automatically prayer but that with intention and by the power of the Spirit everything we do can become prayer when offered faithfully to God.

Wesley gives expression to this complete grace-oriented way of thinking about prayer in *A Plain Account of Christian Perfection*: "All that a Christian does, even in eating and sleeping, is prayer, when it is done in simplicity, according to the order of God, without either adding to or diminishing from it by his own choice."[3] Thinking of prayer in this way brings an orientation to the pastor's life that creates in actuality what is expressed in the language of ordination: that pastors are set apart by the church for, among other things, a life of prayer.

Prayerful Orientation

This is closely connected to the idea, discussed in the previous chapter, that to be a pastor is no career choice; it is an obedient response to the grace of God's call to give oneself over completely to Christ and the church. It means that as a pastor I now live my entire life, every moment and every decision, under the prayerfulness that I am a "symbol among symbols."[4] This means more than giving attention to the reality of my influence over others; it means that my constant orientation toward God shapes my thinking about the gospel and about Christian mission in and for the world. It means that although I may experience many of the mundane realities of life known by all people (work, hunger, loss, happiness, desire, illness, etc.), I can never experience them in any way other than as a pastor whose calling is to name God not only in the life of the church but also in the lives of individuals and in the world. The only way to do this authentically and accurately is to think prayerfully with my whole life. It involves a heightened awareness (maybe a hyperawareness enabled by grace) of the intersections of the gospel and culture.

Pastors see things differently from most other people. We are often misunderstood or simply sidelined socially for this reason. It is also why, as Gordon Lathrop noted, pastors often seem rather sad.[5] This is true, not because we are emotionally depressed or unable to have a good time—pastors certainly know joy and happiness—but because we also, due to this prayerful life, have a continuous awareness of sin's impact on the world. We constantly think of how the gospel and Scripture want to speak to the myriad of dysfunctions we encounter every day, and this is about so much more than working to get up a sermon for Sunday. This is who we are, it's how we think, and it's not really our fault.

It is this life-altering call that God has placed upon us that thrusts us headlong into the ever unfolding collision between the kingdoms of this world and the in-breaking kingdom of God. I think it is what Paul was getting at in his 2 Corinthians 11 description of the ways in which he had known suffering and the burden of ministry. His list of dangers, beatings, and physical abuse is stunning, but his final comment seems in some way to trump every other burden: "Besides everything else, I face daily the pressure of my concern for all the churches" (v. 28). This is the burden of spiritual leadership, the heaviness of responsibility when one assumes the role of pastor among a people. This burden is not about taking upon oneself that which belongs to God, but it is about sharing in the sufferings of Christ (Rom. 8:17). This constant awareness that presses the needs of people toward the hope of the gospel is in essence the prayerfulness that I mean to promote here as thinking prayerfully.

Prayerful Practices

How then does a pastor live into this kind of prayerful life that becomes the foundation for faithful and effective pastoral work? Clearly, the first thing to recognize is that this comes not by our work but by the grace of God. That being said (and it is important to affirm that *all* is by grace), we must do as Charles Wesley wrote, "Come, let us use the grace divine."[6] We do this through the disciplines of space and time, protecting prayer as our first work not only by "going everywhere with Jesus" (a helpful phrase from E. Dee Freeborn[7]) but also by carving out intentional times for retreat from the noise and distractions of contemporary life, following the pattern of our Lord, who "often withdrew to lonely places and prayed" (Luke 5:16). These are deeply intimate, relational, and personal times of communion with the Trinity. They are times different from the pastoral work of intercession or the prayerful attentiveness that connects biblical exegesis with preaching.

This kind of Jesuslike withdrawal is mostly wordless and silent, thus it requires solitude and retreat from the noise of the world. Enjoying this kind of retreat can be as simple as a favorite chair in a corner of my home, sans the temptations of media technologies. I recognize that I am speaking as an introvert who loves solitude, but I remain convinced that this kind of periodic prayerful withdrawal is critical for anyone, regardless of personality or preference, who desires to know God in a way that goes deeper than words.

My father suffered the last seven years of his life under the ravages of dementia. The disease robbed him of words and turned this once articulate and passionate man into a mute. At one point in the journey my sister asked me, "Do you think Dad can still pray?" My response came immediately and, I believe, arose from something deeper than my own thoughts. I heard myself say, "Perhaps now that Dad has no words, he is praying more purely and truly than ever before." It is this deep communion of the Spirit that I am trying to describe as the most essential way to think about what it means for a pastor to be prayerful. These are the "groanings too deep for words" (Rom. 8:26, ESV), which is the promised help of the Holy Spirit, who lifts our very weakness into intercession "according to the will of God" (v. 27, ESV).

Praying in this way is certainly done in solitude, but it is also something that pastors bring into community. Pastoral discipline includes the learned skill of holding everything one does before God in prayerful intention; it means seeking the help of the Spirit in every pastoral encounter so that one's responses are aligned with what the Holy Spirit is seeking to accomplish in the life of an individual or in the life of a community. Hence, pastors are in prayer during counseling sessions, informal conversations, business meetings, and services. Many pastors could testify to the experience of being engaged in a difficult conversation with someone, actively listening while also praying that God would grant wisdom for response. There have been many occasions in my own ministry when I have prayed in that way during a conversation and then heard something come out of my mouth, an insight or advice that I know did not derive entirely from my own knowledge or wisdom. I knew that God was helping me to discern and to articulate truth in such a way that it could be received by the other person. Similar experiences have happened in board meetings, in large-group gatherings and small-group gatherings. It is a way of being that keeps track of the fact that I am never dismissed from pastoral identity and responsibility. My calling is to pay attention, under the help of the Spirit, and to name God in the everyday experiences of people and of communities. This is what it means to think prayerfully.

5

THINKING LEADERSHIP

The idea of leadership is a very important conception for pastoral ministry. Leadership intelligence in any vocation not only involves natural and intuitive abilities but must also involve learned skills and ongoing development. Unfortunately, the idea of leadership and the word itself have suffered gross overuse in popular culture to the point that their significance may be weakened. Over the past thirty years a major industry was birthed around leadership development that now includes nearly numberless conferences, courses, motivational speakers, and books on leadership (especially in airport bookstores!). This focus inevitably found its way to the church, especially into the work of continuing education for pastors. John Maxwell and others introduced the concepts of organizational leadership to pastors and helped many of them improve their skills not only in administration but also in working with lay leaders who spend their days navigating corporate cultures. I want to make sure that I express appropriate esteem for the work of Maxwell and others, because I do believe that they have done something important for church leaders.

Dangers of Leadership Culture

However, the downside of this focus is that it played right into a problem with which pastors are often beset. Many times pastors can easily feel a lack of confidence about their value to a people who have been shaped by modern culture to place highest importance on productivity, power, and success. Consequently, it can be difficult for pastors and laypersons to understand one another with regard to life's priorities. A common joke among pastors is about how laypeople think they only work one day a week. That people really have no idea of what pastors do is understandable. It is hard to describe a life of reflection, prayer, study, and listening to God and God's people in any way that sounds really important. What is especially difficult is helping laypeople understand why in the world anyone would pay someone to do these things. What kind of a job is this, anyway? It really makes no sense in the world's way of reckoning things. So in an attempt to bolster their significance pastors developed job descriptions patterned after those who are esteemed in society: entrepreneurs and executives. We wanted our people to know that we were working hard to run things well, to be on top of things in a way that our organizations would grow and be successful in all the ways that capitalistic societies appreciate.

This is where the language of sociology and business got married to the particular idea of church growth as it developed from the middle twentieth century when Donald McGavran first established the Institute for Church Growth. Again, much about this work was important and needed, but as often happens when movements develop, the markers of this contemporary missionary project got reduced to what many called the ABCs: Attendance, Buildings, and Cash. McGavran evidently saw this and wrote in the preface to the 1980 edition of his book *Understanding Church Growth* (first published in 1970): "Church growth is much wider and deeper than adding names to church rolls. It delves into how persons and peoples become genuinely Christian."[1] This sounds quite contemporary as emerging Christian leaders are moving away from the standards of organizational success toward much more organic and relational ways of thinking about the accomplishing of God's mission in the world. In the meantime, an entire generation of pastoral leaders seemed to take their cues from sources other than, or at least in addition to, the Bible and the church. Many years ago I was profoundly confronted in this regard by the words of Eugene Peterson, who wrote in the introduction to his important book *Working the Angles*:

The pastors of America have metamorphosed into a company of shopkeepers, and the shops they keep are churches. They are preoccupied with shopkeeper's concerns—how to keep the customers happy, how to lure customers away from competitors down the street, how to package the goods so that the customers will lay out more money.[2]

I found myself guilty as charged. In the very first days of leading a congregation, I was greatly tempted to organize my work in ways that would gain me the appreciative recognition of my people. I loved nothing more than hearing people remark about how hard I was working or about what a great job I was doing to "turn this church around," another phrase from the values of business culture. I remember the day I was introduced by a businessman in my congregation to an important bank executive in our city. My church member, a very successful entrepreneur, praised the organizational leadership skill of his new, young pastor. My self-esteem grew as the bank executive nodded his approval, but as we left his office I instinctively knew that something dangerous had just happened. I had succumbed to the powerful temptation to be appreciated and recognized according to the values and priorities of this world.

Biblical Leadership

What I needed, and what my good mentors gave me, was a forceful nudge back to the Scriptures as the basis from which to draw my leadership conceptions. The Bible gives any number of possibilities for this, and many teachers (including those in the organizational leadership culture) have pointed to biblical characters like Joseph, Moses, and Nehemiah as providing models for pastoral leadership. These are helpful lessons, and I have drawn much from them in my own ministry, but I am drawn especially to the life of Jesus as told in the Gospels. These narratives provide the most meaningful way for me to identify the core values that lead to leadership philosophy and practices in harmony with a theology and ethic of self-sacrificing love. As I hear and rehearse the story of Jesus, several key themes seem to emerge, including *humility* (birth in a barn and life as a peasant), *solidarity* (identification with the poor and sick), *compassion* (acts of mercy and healing), *integrity* (no compromise with worldly systems of power), and *sacrifice* (laying down of one's life in service to others). Certainly, other significant components could be named, but these seem to be essential for the shaping of a pastoral theology that is rooted in the life and teaching of Jesus of Nazareth.

Humility calls me to challenge the accepted cultural notion that success is about winning, with the implication that some necessarily lose. Pastors are notoriously competitive when it comes to comparing the alleged scope and significance of our ministries. There is a right expectation that healthy congregations will grow as the community of faith fulfills its role in the mission of God. People will be drawn to churches that live as an authentic expression of the kingdom of God. Often this translates to increased attendance and increased participation in the ministries and programs of the congregation. However, for a pastor to take some kind of personal pride in this Spirit-enabled growth moves more toward the values of this world than toward the values of Jesus. Pastors can enjoy a sense of satisfaction and joy in the fruit of ministry, but if or when this turns to competitive pride, the fruit is in danger of spoil. Humility calls me to account for where and with whom I spend my time as a pastor. To the degree that I begin to prefer the influential and powerful people over the poor and powerless, I am betraying the pattern of Jesus. This is not an either/or proposition; obviously the rich and powerful need the gospel.

The point is that contemporary culture bears such a compelling bias toward the bold and beautiful that pastors must constantly be on guard against neglecting those who often are most difficult to love and serve. This bias can translate to pastors preferring certain posts that enable greater esteem or comfort over posts that could easily be seen (at least in the world's view of things) as lower or less on the scales of importance.

In my work as an overseer, I find myself often working to boost the sense of value and esteem among pastors who are serving faithfully and effectively in posts that regularly pass the notice of others. The Jesus model of humility also reminds me to view every good thing as gift rather than as just reward, which profoundly changes the ethics of work, including how compensation is viewed.

I often hear pastors frame their desire for a decent salary in the form of a moral obligation to provide for their families. In one sense this is hard to argue with, but in another sense where did we ever get the idea that a pastor's compensation should be commensurate with other professionals in the community? This is not to say that congregations have no obligation to support their pastors; clearly, they do and this is biblical. Paul's argument in 1 Corinthians 9 is that "those who preach the gospel should receive their living from the gospel" (v. 14). However, this is in a context whereby Paul does not demand his rights but points to his humble willingness to preach the gospel free of charge. We might also remember the instruction that our Lord gave to his disciples when sending them on mission. Jesus charged them to resist the temptation to secure their own needs and to rely on the hospitality of others, all with the promise of his sending them with "power and authority" (Luke 9:1; see vv. 1-6).

Congregations certainly do have a sacred obligation to provide for support of the ministry, which is a different way of thinking about it than under the normal practices of contractual employment. Contracts are born out of suspicion and mistrust, while covenant relationships are born of love and a mutual commitment to place the needs of the other above one's own needs. I do not mean to suggest that written agreements of expectation between pastors and congregations are wrong, but a covenantal mind-set will go much farther toward establishing heart connections with a people than will a contractual mind-set.

When pastors are considering the call of a congregation to come to their community, it is telling to watch how a candidate handles the question of compensation. Some pastors immediately want to know how much the congregation is ready to pay and how they will support their family. Their decision clearly has much to do with the answer to these questions. Other pastors never ask those questions until after they have accepted the call of the congregation. There are many ways of handling this concern along that continuum, but pastors should be aware of and sensitive to what they communicate to God's people by the way they approach these matters. Regardless of the specific approach chosen, a humble spirit goes a long way toward building a relationship of confidence and trust with a congregation.

Solidarity is closely related to humility and teaches us that our daily decisions, whether critical or mundane, are never chosen in safe isolation but always impact others in ways that we often (perhaps usually) will not see. This has everything to do with joining a people in such a way that they begin to believe and know that the pastor has not just taken a job but is fully casting his or her lot with this particular body of believers. The full embrace of one's assignment moves the pastoral office to a much deeper place than just fulfilling certain functions that the people or the church might expect. It is about willingly and purposefully identifying with congregation and community until the pastor actually belongs to both even while faithfully ordering his or her own life as a prophetic sign of the kingdom of God. This takes a lot of time, and most pastors agree it cannot be done in less than several years.

Authentic solidarity is hard won. It requires repeated episodes of listening to the stories of people, of walking with them through all manner of crises, of navigating and resolving inevitable conflict, and of being there in the everyday rhythms of life until they know that you know and yet you love them anyway. And for this kind of relationship to grow deeply it must be mutual. Pastors must be willing to tell their stories and to be open to reciprocal love. I think of it as *confessional leadership*, which certainly does not mean that I would carelessly display all of my shortcomings. It does mean that I understand my first priority to be a growing disciple of Jesus Christ and then, because of my role in the community, to let others in on that journey of faith. It is the solidarity of sharing together in the cruciform life to which our Lord has called us (Luke 9:23).

Compassion shapes my ethics as it moves me from acts of duty to acts of love. It is one thing (and not necessarily a bad thing) to work for the healing of the lost and broken because I have an ethical obligation to do so. However, the deepest ethical acts of healing seem to rise from a grace-enabled sense of identity with those who suffer. I love the story in Luke's gospel of Jesus encountering the widow of Nain whose only son had died. The death of this son would have left the poor widow utterly destitute. Luke says that when the Lord saw the woman, "his heart went out to her" (Luke 7:13), so he raised the son and gave him back to his mother. Luke's main point is about establishing the authority of Jesus, but one cannot miss the compassion that caused Jesus to interrupt the common scene of a funeral procession with his transforming power. Thinking about leadership in this way means that pastoral compassion is more than a program that I put into place or assignments that I hand out to those under my leadership. It is my personal and passionate involvement in taking the gospel of healing and hope to the broken and marginalized. Pastors lead by getting personally involved as well as by organizing and equipping others for the work of ministry. True compassion demands this personal involvement.

Integrity calls me to account for authentic agreement between my words and my deeds. It's not the idea that I can live out my discipleship flawlessly but that I am always willing to confess my shortcomings and invite others to point out my contradictions so that I might repent and learn. Pastors tend to be fairly poor at this. Part of it may be the unrealistic expectations of our people that we have chosen to embrace. Parishioners are often willing to boost a pastor's sense of spiritual maturity not necessarily because they actually believe the pastor to be spiritually superior but because they are idolatrous. Contemporary Christians don't make golden calves, but they sure do work to cast pastors into a fantasy image of what they imagine a serious Christian to be. Pastoral integrity means working against these idolatrous expectations and demonstrating in word and deed an authentic discipleship that is honest and refuses to think more highly of itself than it ought to think (Rom. 12:3).

The need for accountability will come into view later, but it needs mention here as a significant way for the pastor to resist this kind of congregational idol making. A pastor may have no greater temptation than the heaping of praise and affirmation by an adoring congregation. Certainly, there is a way for congregations to express affirmation and gratitude to and for their pastor without it becoming idolatrous on their part, but even then most pastors need help to make sure they do not begin to draw their identity from any source other than God.

No doubt some pastors reading this are thinking, "That's sure no problem in my church. I'm not their idol but their scapegoat!" Actually, when a congregation refuses to live under pastoral authority and becomes critical and abusive, it is simply the other side of the same idolatry problem. When we realize that our idols cannot deliver what we wanted them to deliver, we turn on them and focus all of our own dysfunction on these symbols of our brokenness. Closely connected to this is the reality that integrity also demands of a pastoral leader that worldly systems of power and influence give way to the Jesus-style power of laying down one's life, which brings the idea of sacrifice into view.

Sacrifice is a decision long before it is an opportunity. It is a mindset that enables one to respond intuitively in a moment of decision in ways that demonstrate a life lived in service to others rather than in protection of one's own interests. The language of servant leadership has gained notice in recent decades through the contributions of Robert Greenleaf and many others. The idea that good leadership looks first toward serving others in ways that enable their growth is a positive impulse and one that is certainly consistent with a pastoral theology formed from the model of Jesus.

The Lord gave us the essential conception of sacrificial leadership when he said, "For even the Son of Man did not come to be served, but to serve, and to give his life as a ransom for many" (Mark 10:45). This is especially instructive for our thoughts about pastoral leadership when we consider the context of Jesus' words. The disciples were in conflict with one another about which of them would be in positions of power and influence in the kingdom of God. Jesus pointed out that they had no idea what they were really asking and moved immediately to the core lesson. True leadership, as Jesus understood and modeled it, is about laying down one's life for the sake of others, acting in the best interest of another, putting one's own concerns in service to the concerns of others.

This kind of orientation for a pastor is much more than a few decisions of service made along the way; it is an entire life orientation that shapes everything about his or her life. It includes the complete surrender to God's will that is expressed by the mother of our Lord when she said, "Let it be to me according to your word" (Luke 1:38, ESV). This is the sense in which any who begin to believe that God is calling them to vocational ministry should give much care and attention to prayer and discernment. No one should embrace the pastoral vocation and the sacrifices involved without a clear vision of God's call. I have often said to students preparing for a life of ministry, "Think carefully and prayerfully on what you are about to do because it will take your life. It will also give you life, but the sacrifices of offering one's life to God and the church are real."

Thinking leadership from the foundational model of Jesus yields an entire philosophy and practice of organizational leadership. It may employ much of the advice of current thinking on leadership dynamics but will always do so within the defining framework of our Lord's mission to serve sacrificially. Many things change when leadership is embraced within this paradigm. Here I am no longer compelled to promote a career but simply move in obedience to the leadership of the Spirit, even when it may appear to be weakness or failure. When relational conflict emerges, as it inevitably will emerge, I can approach resolution from the perspective of sacrificial love and service rather than from a need to win or to be right. I can also release my need to be recognized and appreciated to the larger purposes of serving the mission of God in ways that only eternity will fully reveal.

These qualities of character, which are modeled by our Lord and enabled in us by the work of the Holy Spirit, are closest to the heart of what pastoral leadership means. It would be a good thing if, through the lives of pastors, the very idea of leadership could be recalibrated to have more to do with love than with power. May God give us the courage to lead in this way.

6
THINKING ESSENTIALLY

What are the core and foundational works of a faithful and effective pastor? Answering this question is what I have in mind under the heading of thinking essentially. It is about keeping first things first and rightly understanding what those first things are. The work of pastoring a congregation is complex. One researcher noted that the pastors in his study were able to identify, on average, some 255 separate work activities each averaging fifteen minutes in length.[1] My denominational discipline lists twenty-seven distinct duties under the definition and description of "The Pastor."[2] These duties range from "administer the sacraments" to "submit a report." However, there is some sense of priority given because the list begins with "core duties" and concludes with "administrative duties." The first core duties listed are the following:

1. To pray
2. To preach the Word
3. To equip the saints for the work of ministry
4. To administer the sacraments
5. To care for the people by pastoral visitation, particularly the sick and needy

While this listing may seem correct and right, it is far from assured that pastors will order their lives according to these priorities. Several competing realities can easily conspire to keep a pastor from these essential works. First, the pressing demands of organizational leadership can easily marginalize a pastor into what some have called the tasks of "administrivia."[3] In most posts the pastor is the person who directs the schedule, program, business, and property maintenance of the local church. This carries the potential of scores of contacts, meetings, and errands to make sure that the organization functions properly. It may seem obvious that many of these tasks should be given over to laypersons, but in many settings the expectation of the congregation is that the pastor will give priority to these things. Unless the pastor has a clear understanding of essential things, he or she can easily be seduced by the promise of affirmation when members see their pastor working so hard to run the church. This presents a second conspiring temptation to set aside first things: the desire to be viewed by the congregation as one who is "on top of things" or "astute in matters of business and management" or "working hard to earn the fine salary we pay." Which opens a third competing reality, that if indeed things like prayer, study, and reflection are among the first works of a pastor, only the pastor can really provide the discipline needed to protect the required space to attend to these things. Expressions of expectation, disappointment, or frustration from laypeople rarely come because we are not praying enough or reading enough. Such expressions nearly always come because we are not meeting the demands of organizational leadership or because we somehow failed to meet their particular expectation in some way. The regular accountability of collegial fellowship is important at this point.

Vision for First Things

Several years ago the congregation I was serving as pastor gave me one of the greatest gifts I have ever received. The congregation gave to me and my family a seven-week sabbatical to break completely away from the daily tasks of ministry. In addition to the precious time with my family, those weeks gave me a chance to work on an essential question, "What am I really supposed to be doing?" The question always seemed to lurk in the back of my mind, but in the newly opened space of sabbatical the question thrust itself to the forefront of my thinking in various forms: "What is a pastor? How does a pastor live and work? When does a pastor say yes and when does a pastor say no?"

Gladly, the Bible speaks to these questions explicitly and implicitly. During the sabbatical I went again to the obvious texts, reading the Pastoral Epistles over and over again. I studied the pastoral theology of 2 Corinthians. I noted the pattern of the apostles in Acts. I considered the leadership models of Moses, Ezekiel, Nehemiah, Jesus, and others. As I did this, a fresh clarity began to emerge in my mind and heart about what a pastoral leader is to be and to do. I simply made lists of indicative and imperative statements as each set of texts were studied.

There were pages of notes, but reflection revealed that authentic pastoral work really boils down to a few essential activities. These themes are repeated so often there is simply no mistaking their import. Pastors are to study so that they can preach and teach the Scriptures rightly. Pastors are to pray, listening to the Spirit and engaging in intercession. Pastors are to listen to the people under their charge, giving wise counsel and spiritual direction. Pastors are to set an example for the flock. I believe that nearly all pastors would affirm these things as essential to their work. I also believe that nearly all pastors know how easy it is to be sidetracked from these core duties and find themselves spending their best energy and time in tasks that do not necessarily seem to strike at the heart of their calling.

My thinking about essential things is profoundly shaped by Eugene Peterson through his book *Working the Angles*.[4] Here, Peterson suggests that the simple image of a triangle can be instructive in how we think about essential things. When looking at a triangle, we notice the lines in relationship to one another, but what gives particular shape to those lines that we call it a triangle are the angles. Peterson says that in pastoral ministry the noticeable lines are the public acts such as preaching and teaching, visitation, and administration. The angles, however, are those works that actually give a true pastoral ministry its shape. These angles are the essential works of prayer, study of the Scriptures, and giving spiritual direction to people through prayerful and reflective listening. This is a brief summary of his thesis, but thinking about these three foundational works forms the heart of what I want to say to developing ministers about thinking essentially.

Prayer

Prayer as the first essential work of a pastor may seem obvious. However, most experienced pastors would confess that keeping prayer at the center of their work is anything but easy. Chapter 4 gave focus to the most central aspect of pastoral prayer, the constancy of a prayerful mind and heart throughout one's life and work. Here the focus moves from that center to the particular works of prayer that are essential in order for true pastoral ministry to emerge. Two broad categories may be helpful to organize these thoughts about the work of prayer. One is what I would call the prayers of solitude, meaning the ways in which a pastor prays in private, going into the closet of prayer (Matt. 6:6). The other category is public prayer or prayer in the midst of the community gathered for worship and fellowship.

Pastoral prayer that takes place in solitude seems to me among the most beautiful of pastoral works and among the truest of ways for a pastor to love his or her people. Prior to praying in this way as pastoral service, however, is the discipline of going to the prayer closet that we might learn how to pray. Therefore, much of this way of praying is about entering the kind of silence that Elijah came to know in the painful intensity of his post-Carmel desert experience (1 Kings 19). God did not speak to Elijah at Mount Horeb in the ways we might expect God to speak. Not in the wind that "tore the mountains" or in earthquake or in fire. We often hope for a spectacular sign of God's speaking, but the text says after all of these impressive signs there was just a "low whisper" or "thin silence" (v. 12, ESV margin). The narrative does not say that God was in the silence but that from the silence Elijah was able to hear the voice of God. In the life of the church prayer is so often connected to words that we are tempted to forget the deepest way of prayer is born of silence. When Christians do not pray well, it may often be attributed to a failure to begin well by creating the necessary space for prayer. Our temptation is to rush right into the words and consequently to fill our ears with our own voice rather than the ability to hear God.

Although the deepest ways of prayer are settled in silence, prayer as pastoral work would also move toward intercession. I think Peterson has it right when he notes that prayer is "answering speech," always in response to God who is speaking.[5] This awareness brings great confidence in prayer, knowing that as we pray for our people, we are simply joining God's reach of grace toward them. In intercession we are not begging God to do something that God does not want to do. Rather, we are learning to hear God's voice in such clarity that our will becomes molded to the will of God. In this way of praying, it is wise for us to learn to use the language of God's people in prayer through the centuries. Prayerful Christians have always turned to the Psalms, the prayer book of God's covenant people, to give them language for prayer that they may not otherwise know. The soaring speech of praise given to us in the Psalms provides opportunity for rich expressions of worship beyond what we might know left to our own limited words. The psalmist's expressions of lament give comfort and hope to the suffering. The Lord seemed to pray the Psalms in this way, quoting, for example, Psalm 22 from the cross. Even imprecatory psalms offer a language for prayer in the midst of persecution that gives the prayerful Christian a way of expressing thoughts and feelings that are not always *nice,* in the popular and sentimental use of that term. Perhaps one of the worst things that happened to me in my church upbringing was being taught to talk nice to God, effectively placing God at an arm's length, like the distancing politeness of greeting a stranger. The point is that pastors, in order to be faithful and effective pastors, must go deep into the school of prayer where the main text is the hymnbook of Israel. Others have written deeply on this subject, and their work can guide the pastor in this important component of pastoral life.[6]

Alongside Psalms as a guide to prayer are also the prayers of the church. These include the prayers offered to the worshipping community in liturgies and guides to prayer, such as the Book of Common Prayer. These prayers, while mostly prayed together in worship, can also link the prayers in cell to the life of the church. Coming under the teaching of the church on prayer would also include the prayers of the saints throughout the centuries, not only learning from but also offering as our own prayer the expressions of those who have gone before. It is remarkable, when done with intention and attention, how these ancient and communal prayers can begin to shape the prayer life of a Christian and of a pastor.

Sabbath keeping is an important part of this discussion on the prayers of solitude. Chapter 9 will focus on the practices of Sabbath in the life of pastor and congregation, but a quick note here may serve to remind us that learning well the deep lessons of prayer requires adequate spaces of place and time. These kinds of spaces are only fully afforded by obeying the God-created rhythm of work and rest. Pastors tend to be chief among Sabbath breakers, excusing their failure as a necessary consequence of the relentless demands of pastoral work. The idea that I do not have time to observe the Sabbath principle because of the importance of my work is a destructive lie that bears the seeds of total vocational failure. This is not about "taking a day off"; it is something much deeper and more important. It is about embracing the most essential work of a Christian that is also the most essential work of a pastor: building the foundation for a truly prayerful life.

Public prayer is the most dangerous kind of prayer. Jesus warned us about this with his words about prayer in the Sermon on the Mount (Matt. 6:5-13). The focus of this text is not about a condemnation of public prayer. Jesus is teaching us to be honest and careful about our hearts when we pray. He is warning against careless prayer. The Lord says that two things must be avoided in order for prayer to be authentic. The first is praying to impress others, and the second is praying to impress God. The problem in either case is that we forget to whom we are talking. Pastors praying in the worshipping community of faith and leading the congregation in prayer is certainly important, but it is also a dangerous temptation to pray impressively, passionately, or manipulatively. This is why careful preparation for pastoral prayer in worship is so important. The challenge is to avoid simply praying *for* the people but rather to lead the people in praying. Liturgies of the prayers of the people can be very helpful.

Pastors are often called upon to pray in other gatherings where prayer seems the appropriate, if not obligatory, thing to do. In one sense this is a fine opportunity for pastors to name God's presence in the midst of God's people and in communities, but it can also be perilous if pastors are not extremely careful with these opportunities, resisting the tendency of people to try and control God by domesticating the presence of God's servant. The only way to avoid this is for the pastor to be so immersed in the first work of prayer that even when called upon in a token way to "offer a prayer," the people under the hearing of the prayer are compelled to confess that this minister has been with God. This is not about the words; it is about the presence of the Spirit, who anoints faithful prayer with the power of God.

Scripture Study

The idea that pastors would study Scripture may be obvious to everyone. However, I want to suggest that there is a way of doing it that is probably not obvious to everyone. Too often pastors approach Scripture as something to be mastered, understood, mined for truth, or worse, just to "find something to preach." Years ago I heard Millard Reed, a great pastor and educator in the Church of the Nazarene, liken this to the precarious effort of cracking open a walnut without damaging the meat. The possibility is to become so impatient with the careful and persistent tapping that we finally finish the job with one sharp blow of the exegetical hammer, only to find ourselves left with several rather unsatisfying pieces of what was once a beautiful whole.

Scripture study for the pastor is about so much more than opening a complex text or mastering content. The real danger here is that we put everything up in the head and fail to hear God's voice in the study. The Bible is not a textbook; it is living by the power of the Spirit as the risen Christ speaks to us again and again in its reading, study, and hearing. We do not listen to Scripture only to figure out what God said once upon a time but to hear God speaking to the church. This is why understanding Scripture in a narrative way, or as the story of God, is so essential to the pastoral work of helping our people to engage the living Word. God is still telling a story, and we are involved in the unfolding of that story. Consequently, the pastoral work of Scripture study is largely about the text, under the anointing of the Spirit, doing its work first on the preacher so that proclamation rises from a whole life, not just from the mind. This is not to dismiss careful and accurate exegesis: studying language, context, and culture. We access pertinent resources to understand how the text sought to function in shaping God's people and how it seeks still to function as a fresh word from the Lord. This work is important and necessary; it's just not the whole thing. The work of study is inexorably linked to prayer so that the pastor is immersed in the conversation that the Holy Spirit has created throughout the life of the church and is still creating as the pastor works to "break the bread of life" in the midst of the congregation.

Doing this work well implies a great amount of time. This kind of study cannot be rushed, which is not to comment only on the number of hours spent each week in study but to include one's whole life and experience in the ongoing development of capacities for exegesis and teaching. In other words, what pastors bring to the pulpit on Sunday is so much more than the work of that particular week or month. Thoughtful pastors bring all of life as well as the teaching of the church over time to speak through a particular text to a particular context in Spirit-inspired ways that become for the people of God a life-giving word from the Lord.

I am aware in writing this of the unique burden that is constantly carried by bivocational pastors who would love the chance to linger in the study. I confess that I do not have personal experience in this difficult work, but I would still encourage my bivocational colleagues and all of us to resist the temptation simply to take another's sermon as our own work. Even if we must rely heavily on the exegetical and even homiletical work of another (which is not in and of itself inappropriate), we must go beyond simply reciting a sermon. We must allow the truth of the work to go into our hearts, to wrestle prayerfully with our own response to the Word, and then to preach the sermon, not with borrowed passion, but from authentic and personal engagement. It is not terribly meaningful for pastors to think about (less to talk about) how many hours each week they spend in sermon preparation. Certainly, we must give some quantity and quality to this central work, but the truth is that sermon preparation, when borne from a life of Scripture study as one of the core pastoral works, is a constant activity that is never really completed.

Spiritual Direction

One would assume this to be at the very heart of pastoral work, but as Eugene Peterson says, "Too many pastors only dabble in spiritual direction."[7] This is not entirely our fault, for contemporary pastors have been steeped in a culture that prefers the quick and the instant. Spiritual direction, like the essential works of prayer and study, requires a process that takes a lot of time. Again Peterson says, "It is easier to tell people what to do than to be with them in a discerning, prayerful companionship as they work it out."[8] The idea of sharing life with people in this way places it at odds with almost everything else about contemporary American culture. Our people are so busy that they hardly have time to linger in conversation with the people in their own households, much less the people in their congregation or their pastor. And, truthfully, pastors are sometimes so distracted by the "busyness" of ministry that they do not have time really to listen to folks—and they know it. Our lack of confidence or perhaps lack of clarity about our call causes us to talk too much about how busy we are and how hard we are working to run the church. When we do this, we certainly do not inspire confidence in our people that we are able or even interested in attending to their lives.

Pastors may also need to be careful about how they use social media in ministry. While the instruments of social media are tremendous tools for many aspects of our connection to people, there is a way of caring that demands a kind of presence that simply cannot be achieved fully through tweet, post, or text. The art of spiritual direction is about more than giving advice. It is significantly about the flesh-and-blood ministry of being with people, sitting with them, and actively listening to them.

Attending to souls (spiritual direction) is mostly about listening. It is not only listening to another but being with and guiding another as both you and that person listen to God. I believe that some of my best pastoral work was done when I said nothing, or at least very little, but actively listened to someone. By active listening, I mean posturing in ways that express engagement, making eye contact, putting away distractions (read "turn off cell phone"), and occasionally repeating back what you are hearing the other say. In these ways and in a world like ours where this kind of listening is in such short supply, a pastor (as any Christian) can achieve what I think Mary Rose O'Reilly was referring to when she wrote, "One can, I think, listen someone into existence."[9] If ever you have loved people in this way and witnessed the transformation of soul that begins to happen when they know that they are being heard, not only in the words they are speaking but in their very heart, then you know that this observation is true. By the help of the Spirit, a kind of resurrection of spirit can happen in the deadened souls of people who for myriad of reasons stopped believing somewhere along the way that they had anything of value to offer to God and the world. This is not necessarily the kind of work that gets noticed in pastors' reports and conferences, but it is at the core of a faithful pastor's essential work.

There is another important way that spiritual direction happens when we may not be aware that it is happening. It is the shaping work that takes place not because we are speaking something directly into persons' lives but because they are watching us, looking to see if something in our lives is worthy of imitation. A pastor does well to remember that when he or she is the spiritual leader of a congregation, there is never a time when he or she is not the pastor. This is certainly not to suggest that a pastor only plays a role and that we must always be "on" as performers or play actors. That kind of existence is shallow and unsustainable. What it means is that whether we are functioning in direct pastoral duties or fulfilling other life roles (spouse, parent, neighbor, patron, citizen, etc.), we can never imagine that we are not being watched to see how a mature Christian lives. This is the other side of the coin to the idolatry problem mentioned in the last chapter, and it is an important component. While we must resist people casting us as idols, we also must take seriously our responsibility to give spiritual direction through the witness of our entire lives. The way we manage our time, our resources, our relationships, and our health all get to be a part of the way we lead our people. It's the courageous and yet humble invitation that the apostle Paul extends to the Corinthians: "Be imitators of me, as I am of Christ" (1 Cor. 11:1, ESV).

Prayer, Scripture study, and spiritual direction are the core and essential works of a faithful and effective pastor. Pastors do many other things, of course, and therein is the danger. The constant threat is to become overrun with secondary things rather than keeping the focus on first things. The good news is that when these essential works are given their rightful place, they become generative in a pastor's life in such a way that there seems an adequate resource of energy and even time to do the other tasks of ministry. My accountability partner regularly prays for me that God will "expand the time" so that I can accomplish what I feel called by God to accomplish. Obviously, God does not answer that prayer by changing how time works, but God does answer the prayer by helping me to resist what is urgent and live toward what is truly important. This is thinking essentially.

7

THINKING HUMBLY

A humble bearing in the life of a pastor begins with the recognition that nothing about vocational ministry is earned; it is a gift in every way. One of the critical ways this works out into pastoral life is through an evident attitude of submission to God and to the authority of the church. My work with hundreds of developing ministers over the years has confirmed that this kind of humility and submissive bearing can never be taken for granted. It is grace, but it is also a spiritual discipline and a learned posture.

Ordination Not Earned

The requirements for ordained ministry are substantive, as they should be. Not only do we have the daunting New Testament descriptions of Christian leadership character and practices (1 Tim. 3, for example), but also most churches set forth prerequisites for education, training, service, and evaluation that require a process of several years. In my denomination there is a prescribed course of study that requires at least a three- to four-year period to complete and is often much longer. Other denominations require a master of divinity degree, which usually requires at least three years beyond undergraduate study. There is also a licensing process for the discernment of the church that requires a number of years before a person could even be considered for ordination, including an annual evaluation of the person's development by the elders of the church. Then there is a period of service in the local church requiring, at minimum, three years for a congregation of God's people to help discern grace and gifts for ministry in a candidate.

It is not difficult to imagine, then, that having completed these steps, and having checked these items off the list, that candidates might have the idea that the church is now obligated to ordain them. They would be wrong. The humility that ordained life requires begins with the surrender of a "rights" orientation to the embrace of a servant orientation. I serve if, when, and wherever the church calls me to serve, having surrendered control of my life to the will of God as expressed through the will of the church.

Downward Mobility

I recognize that these are hard and perhaps offensive words, especially to American Christians who imagine individual rights as something God-given and inalienable. If, however, the question of the ownership of one's life is not settled right here, one will be in for a long experience of frustration and disappointment. The way of the kingdom of God, as Henri Nouwen wisely noted, is not upward mobility but that of downward mobility. This idea rises from his personal journal kept during the year between leaving his Harvard post and arriving at the L'Arche community of Daybreak in Canada. On the way, Nouwen spent a year in a home for people with mental handicaps in Trosly-Breuil in France. He spent considerable time taking care of Adam, one of the residents, who taught him profound lessons of the way of Jesus. Nouwen defines it in this way:

> Every time Jesus speaks about being glorified and giving glory, he always refers to his humiliation and death. It is through the way of the cross that Jesus gives glory to God, receives glory from God, and makes God's glory known to us. The glory of the resurrection can never be separated from the glory of the cross. The risen Lord always shows us his wounds. Thus the glory of God stands in contrast to the glory of the people. People seek glory by moving upward. God reveals his glory by moving downward. If we truly want to see the glory of God, we must move downward with Jesus.[1]

The remarkable thing about Nouwen's testimony is that his notion of this downward mobility was more than an attitude or way of thinking; it was actionable. He lived it out by choosing to move away from assignments seen as important or esteem-building to assignments that may appear as menial or even degrading. This way of serving stands in stark contrast to what I sometimes witness among pastors. Interaction with pastors who are seeking assignment suggests to me that concerns about where one is assigned often revolve largely around the perceived prestige of the post that arises from the size of the congregation or its reputation as a desirable location. These concerns are connected to the ability of the congregation to provide a decent salary, which is an understandable and legitimate concern particularly when the minister is trying to support a family. However, there is a peril here that must be navigated carefully by the pastor who truly seeks to work from a servant orientation.

The danger is that decisions about the sense of God's call and leading to particular assignments could be shaped more by the practical concerns of compensation or reputation than by faithfully executing one's calling. This is not to suggest that the humble pastor would never be able to include questions of provision for his or her family in these decisions. There is a way, however, to engage these concerns without allowing them to cloud the possibility that God's call may and often does include the embrace of assignments that are not the most comfortable or attractive. Doing this well involves something of a subtlety that requires much prayer and the strong accountability of spiritual directors, including friends, family, and colleagues.

I mentioned earlier that I am always interested to see when in the process of pastoral call the candidate raises the practical questions of compensation, benefits, parsonage, and so forth. Some pastors want to know the answer to these questions very early and sometimes withdraw from the process when they learn the answers. Others never ask the questions until they have already been elected to serve, believing that if God calls, God will provide. Many others, of course, fall somewhere along that continuum. The real concern here is that pastors must live and work from an attitude of humility rather than of self-promotion, pride, or acquisition for its own sake. In one sense, no one enters pastoral ministry in order to make money; it is not generally known as a lucrative position. Many pastors are so gifted, experienced, and educated that they could do quite well in other careers. Nevertheless, we must guard our hearts in this regard whether that means guarding from avarice or guarding from bitterness. In either case, humility calls us to the surrender of both our own imagined rights and those supported by the cultures (both popular and ecclesial) around us. Pastors would do well to inculcate the words of Thomas à Kempis:

> Strive . . . to do another's will rather than thine own. Choose always to have less rather than more. Seek always after the lowest place, and to be subject to all. Wish always and pray that the will of God be fulfilled in thee. Behold, such . . . as this entereth into the inheritance of peace and quietness.[2]

Submission to Authority

Another critical aspect of pastoral humility is a submissive attitude toward authority. This plays out in several ways. First, the life of every Christian is lived in submission to the authority of God. What is easily confessed, however, can be much harder actually to live. Christians are known to bargain with God all the time over the unreasonable expectations of a cruciform life. A life offered in submission to God will mean the evident embrace of the upside-down values of the kingdom of God. For example, Jesus calls those who would be first to become last, those who would be served to serve, and those who would gain life to lose their lives for the sake of the gospel.

Measuring these values against the realities of my own life causes very hard questions to be pressed into my heart. Am I really willing to serve where God has placed me when it looks to everyone else like I am accepting failure? Am I really willing to serve where God has placed me when it results in my own suffering, or worse, in suffering for my loved ones? Am I really willing to serve where God has placed me when the opportunity for a better post comes along? A pastor must be careful with these questions, answering them honestly and selflessly. Too many pastors have dragged their spouses and families into difficult situations more from their own hubris than from faith. However, this can work both ways. Sometimes faithfulness takes pastors to assignments that clearly are good for their families. Other times, faithfulness to God may call a pastor's sanity into question. The career decisions that a cruciform life requires will make very little if any sense to most people who watch and wonder why in the world anyone would do such a thing. A spiritual bearing of authentic humility is the only way to make sense of such a life.

A critical component of a pastor's submission to God's authority is the attitude and practices of submission to ecclesial authorities. From the beginning, the church has understood the necessity of spiritual authority being reflected in the organization of the people of God for mission and ministry. This cannot be reduced to organizational leadership theory but must remain vitally connected to the idea of submission to God's authority as foundational for mature discipleship. Scripture clearly establishes human relationships as a matter of submitting to godly authority. It may be expressed between husbands and wives, parents and children, or slaves and masters, but the graced ability to come under the mission of another in loving service is an essential Christian posture. Hebrews 13:17 applies it to the relationship between God's people and their pastors: "Have confidence in your leaders and submit to their authority, because they keep watch over you as those who must give an account. Do this so that their work will be a joy, not a burden, for that would be of no benefit to you."

Amazingly, God has called us to submit to the authority of our spiritual leaders, knowing that they are fallible and flawed. Evidently, God trusts the vitality of God's church to imperfect leaders. Every pastor is aware that one day he or she will stand before God and give account for his or her ministry. This text also suggests that God's people may be called to give account for how they treated their spiritual leaders. Could this suggest that all of us will be called to account for our willingness and ability to submit to those in authority over us? I pray that no Christian or congregation comes under the judgment of God because of disobedience to this clear biblical instruction.

In the same way, pastors must learn to submit to those in authority over them—that is, the overseers (*episkopoi*) of Christ's church. Whenever pastors assume an adversarial role with those in authority over them, it harms the witness of the church and undermines their own pastoral authority. Too often the language of pastors moves in this direction. This is certainly not to suggest that church leaders are beyond questioning or accountability; this is not and must not ever be the case. All of us are under authority. However, all with authority validate their leadership character and integrity by demonstrating in their own lives the willingness and ability to come under the authority of others. I recognize that this is coming from one who currently serves the church in the role of superintendent. The polity manual of my denomination regularly employs the language of "due regard" in describing this idea of appropriate submission to authority. The charge is given to pastors in this way: "The pastor shall always show due regard for the united advice of the district superintendent and the District Advisory Board."[3] A similar charge is given to the district superintendent to show due regard for general superintendents. This is just one way, and not the only way, in which the spiritual grace of humility is to function in the lives of pastors.

Humble Leadership Posture

There is another aspect of this critical humility whereby pastors are accountable to their congregations, the very people they have been called to lead and to serve. Similarly, overseers in the church are accountable back to the church not only through the judicial processes of election and governance but especially in the manner of Christlike humility. The way this gets expressed is through a demeanor that is neither grasping nor demanding. This leadership posture is both collaborative and confessional.

By *collaborative* I mean working with the people under our authority in such a way that they know without doubt that they have a key role to play in the fulfillment of the overall mission. There is a fine balance here of casting vision and leading the way but also of not acting as though we are the only ones who know what to do or how to do it. Consequently, this is largely about listening well and authentically taking into account the ideas and offerings of those under our leadership, even when our impulse may be to discount or disagree. One temptation that pastors need to check is the referencing of past ministries, especially in the earlier days of establishing their leadership in a new place. This can be expressed in many ways but often sounds as simple as, "Well, back in Frog Jump we did it this way." The things that worked well in Frog Jump may in fact be useful in the new location, but constant reference to other experiences or contexts does not inspire confidence in the people that their pastor is taking them seriously as partners in ministry.

Another challenge of working in a collaborative way comes when the congregation has developed a mind-set that the pastor is a sort of hired hand to take care of the facilities as well as the services of the church. Changing this is difficult, having been reinforced by far too many well-meaning pastors, but it can be done over time through careful teaching from the Scriptures about the meaning of the pastoral office and the nature of the body of Christ expressed in congregations.

By *confessional* I mean to suggest something about how those under our leadership learn about our character in ways that build the critical factor of trust. This is closely connected to the idea of leading in a collaborative way and has to do with a sense of personal confidence that is not threatened by the success of those under our leadership and actually celebrates and enjoys their victories. Confessional leadership is the willingness to allow people to see weaknesses and shortcomings as well as strengths and skills, not in any manipulative way, but simply by living authentically as a member of the community of faith. This way of leading is all about integrity that calls us to account for authentic agreement between our words and our deeds. It is an offered accountability that actually invites others to point out our contradictions so that we might repent and learn. In this kind of confessional leadership, worldly systems of power and influence give way to the cruciform model of laying down one's life in service to Christ and the church. I know this kind of leadership bearing is quite different from what is usually celebrated in the ubiquitous literature on leadership. Talking this way will have people looking at you crossways, questioning your intelligence and skill. It is not born of cool leadership strategy but of genuine surrender to the Jesus-style leadership of laying down one's life.

These descriptions bring to mind one more significant way in which a humble bearing is demonstrated in the life of the pastor: the commitment to remain. I will mention two ways of doing this, although more could no doubt be named. The first sense of it is in persistence, not only in vocational ministry but also in a particular assignment. In the sixth century of the church, Benedict added a fourth vow to the traditional ordination vows of poverty, chastity, and obedience: the vow of stability. This was the commitment of pastors to remain where God and the church had placed them even when (maybe especially when) the place was not very pleasing to them. Why would this be important? Consider the contrast of the constant and faithful pastor with the contemporary habit of short, serial relationships that are so much a part of life in our time. If the pastor is truly to be a "symbol among symbols" as Gordon Lathrop noted, what better way to model God's faithfulness than through a vocational life that does not capriciously move from place to place or throw in the towel when the going gets a bit rough? I am keenly aware that remaining is not always a decision of the pastor. We have too many stories of pastors being forced out of assignments by idolatrous congregations. I have in mind here those times when it is a pastor's decision whether to remain or to leave, and having a humble bearing is critical in helping make this decision well.

Another sense of remaining is in a word I want to offer especially to my young friends. I noted in the introduction to this book an "emerging generation of pastoral leaders who dare to name what is broken about the church." We need these voices, but too many of them are distancing themselves or being distanced by leaders who really do not want to hear what they have to say. My appeal to these young leaders is to remain. As I said earlier, don't be afraid of the risk of being labeled a conformist or whatever else could convince you that there is no place for you at this table.[4] The question of breaking fellowship with a particular part of the church is something with which John Wesley wrestled as one committed to the Church of England yet working for its revival. He was deeply concerned about what he called *schism* or anything that tore at the unity of the body of Christ. Wesley's sermon under the title "On Schism" includes this passionate plea:

Do not rashly tear asunder the sacred ties which unite you to any Christian society . . . Take care how you rend the body of Christ by separating . . . Separation is a thing evil in itself. It is a sore evil in its consequences . . . Do not lay more stumbling blocks in the way of these for whom Christ died.[5]

The only exceptions Wesley seemed to tolerate had to do with those rare instances where a particular body would require its pastor to do something that Scripture forbids or if one were being required to omit something that Scripture clearly commands. Sharing his own contemporary struggles at this point, Thomas Oden writes, "Wesley warned against becoming trapped in a syndrome of impatience, anger, and resentment against the received historic church."[6] These are wise words from spiritual men that I intend to heed in my own life offered to Christ and the church, and I would urge my young friends in ministry to submit to the authority of this truth and by God's grace to remain.

These attitudes, this way of thinking, and this kind of vocational bearing are what I mean by *thinking humbly*. There is nothing easy about it and certainly nothing weak or wanting in this way of executing one's ministry. It is the way of Jesus, and it is a way that even while requiring the laying down of one's life, brings life, peace, and joy.

8
THINKING HOLY

As a book under the category of practical theology, I certainly want this work to be practical, and the latter half will move more in that direction. However, it seems to me that to launch right into thoughts about pastoral tasks, strategies, or parish responsibilities would be to jump into the middle of the conversation rather than to work at the beginning. In this first part I have tried to begin with issues of pastoral character and heart. Taking to account all that has been said so far, nothing encompasses the heart of a faithful and effective pastor more than the rich, biblical idea of holiness. Saying this may reveal that I am here speaking of holiness most essentially from the idea of love rather than first from the idea of sanctification or purity. Clearly, holiness and sanctification are not to be separated, but I am thinking here especially of the relationship of pastor and people that may become a conduit of God's grace expressed in holy love. The most important thing to say about pastoral life and work is something about holiness: the laying down of one's life for the sake of others.

Relational Holiness

I certainly do not intend to attempt a thorough holiness theology here, being far beyond the scope of this work and my own ability. However, I do want to think about how the biblical idea of holiness and the Wesleyan expression of "holiness of heart and life" play out in the life and ministry of a pastor. This should never be taken for granted. It is possible for ministries to be shaped more by pastors seeking to be served rather than to serve. For most of my ministerial life I have heard some elders in ministry bemoan a loss of respect that once was paid to pastors by people and by culture generally. I understand this desire for respect, but I am also troubled by it. Respect for the pastoral office is spiritually crucial and necessary, but deference to a particular Christian who happens to hold a respectable office is dangerous. It is dangerous both for the person to whom it is given and for the community that gives it. The danger for the person is that he or she could be tempted to think of himself or herself "more highly than you ought" (Rom. 12:3). The danger for the community is that it could be tempted to make an idol out of the very one that God appointed to serve as a lowly shepherd who cares for the sheep.

One way that holiness of heart and life becomes evident in the life of a leader is through surrender of the expectation that he or she will enjoy honor, preference, or deference because of his or her role in the church. A desire to be served rather than to serve can be revealed when pastors seek to position themselves as being beyond questioning, beyond accountability, or beyond correction. I have already argued that the idea of submission to authority is important in the Christian life, but this is not to say that a pastor should come to expect or demand this submissive posture from his or her people. When respect and submission are given, they must be received humbly and quietly as wonderful gifts of grace. If ever I come to think that I am entitled to these things because I hold the office of pastor, I begin to betray the essence of holiness of heart and life.

Perhaps nowhere is the temptation to be served more evident than in times of congregational conflict. This will be a point of focus in chapter 15, but for now suffice it to say that too often pastors succumb to the temptation during conflict to win at all costs, rather than to demonstrate a willingness to slow down, back off, listen more carefully, and sometimes to change their course for the sake of a greater communal good. These moves are much more, or should be more, than deftly applied leadership strategies. They should emerge from a deeply known reception of God's sanctifying grace so that one's will more and more easily gives way to steadfast obedience to the will of God. This represents a way of thinking and being that is in stark contrast to the accepted ways of this world. This way can also be in contrast to the ways of leading that congregations sometimes come to desire from their pastors—the idea that our leader would be a kind of king in the manner of other kings who run their organizations with power and decisive action. What I am placing in contrast to this kind of command and control leadership is not weak or uncertain leadership but a leadership that is so defined by God's perfect love that it no longer has anything of its own to prove; it has only to prove the authenticity of a love that lays down its life in service to another. This is what I mean by *thinking holy.*

The idea of laying down one's life in service to others is not only about serving people and meeting their needs. I am thinking especially of what it means for a pastor to become a living sign among the people of God's transforming grace, which is not something different from laying one's life down in service to others. Part of embracing a "living sacrifice" (Rom. 12:1) way of life is the modeling of a transformed life that does not "conform to the pattern of this world" (v. 2). We pastors seem to focus so much on how to preach holiness and teach holiness. These are important foci, but I am suggesting that what we especially need are pastors who model in daily life the way of holiness. This becomes evident far beyond the religious activities of a pastor, but even more when a pastor in the entirety of life demonstrates what holiness of heart and life looks like day by day. It is about a pastor giving first and best energies to the life of becoming more and more like Christ in the whole of life, out of which flow the activities of teaching, caring, and leading a congregation.

Follow Me . . . Follow Christ

Many years ago I stood before a congregation that was considering calling me to be their pastor. The superintendent asked me to respond to a question that is common in that sort of setting. The question was, "What is your philosophy of ministry?" I said several things in answer to the question, but first from my mouth was this response: "My first responsibility as a pastor is to be a growing, maturing disciple of Jesus Christ. And then, because of my unique role in the congregation, to allow the people to see my journey and to learn something there about what it means to be a fully surrendered, sanctified follower of Jesus." I spent fourteen years of my life and ministry seeking to do just that in the midst of that same congregation. There is no way I would suggest that I did so flawlessly, for they know better! However, reflecting on those fourteen years as their pastor I have no doubt that my influence on them for good went far beyond my preaching, teaching, or administration. I lived life before them not only as a pastor but also as a husband, father, son, friend, and citizen. Fencing off my life from view of the people is not a faithful way of being pastor. My people need not only to hear biblical and theological truth about holiness but also to see how a serious Christian seeks to live it out by the grace of God.

The expressed theology of ordination of my denomination states in part, "Ordination bears witness to the Church universal and the world at large that this candidate evidences an exemplary life of holiness."[1] This is not to say something unique to clergy. The charge to "seek earnestly to perfect holiness of heart and life in the fear of the Lord"[2] is given to every member, but it bears specific mention here because pastors should be replicable models of what this means. Somehow, the pursuit of holiness must become much more than words spoken in a sermon or even in a personal testimony. The pursuit of holiness needs to become obvious in the life of pastors in such a way that the people are encouraged to believe in transforming grace and challenged to use the grace that is given in their own lives. This is something much deeper than any strategy or even spiritual discipline. This is a way of following Jesus that shapes one's core being so profoundly that Christlikeness becomes the only adequate way to describe that kind of life. It's the kind of recognition mentioned in Scripture when the religious elders of Israel observed something unique about Peter and John; the elders "took note" that although these two men were ordinary, they "had been with Jesus" (Acts 4:13). Again, this is not unique to pastors, as all Christians are called to become exemplars of holiness, but this kind of Jesus following forms the center of what it means to be a pastor for and in the midst of a congregation and community. Andrew Purves, reflecting on the writings of Gregory of Nazianzus, writes, "The pastor, as soul of the congregation, is given the extraordinary task of sharing in the work of . . . making godly the people of God."[3]

A Beautiful Mind

This discussion may seem to belong under the title *Being* Holy, but I place it here under the title *Thinking* Holy, in the sense of Romans 12:2, where we read in part, "be transformed by the renewing of your mind." The holy life to which God calls us and for which God has made provision in the death and resurrection of Jesus has much to do with how we think—a renewal of our mind by grace that enables us to live individually (holy persons) and together (holy church) as bright testimony to God's redemptive purposes for the world. How we think is revealed in our words and actions. Consequently, holiness of heart (mind) and life, or its lack, will become evident in how pastors talk and how pastors order their lives. This is a word of exhortation and perhaps correction to pastors living in a time when our senses are flooded with words. As a pastor, does my speech simply reflect the shrill and panicked voices of contemporary culture? Is holiness at work in me in such a way that my speech models an alternative possibility for my congregation and community? This kind of holy, life-giving speech would be characterized by the fruit of the Spirit: "love, joy, peace, forbearance, kindness, goodness, faithfulness, gentleness and self-control" (Gal. 5:22-23). When the fruit of the Spirit is finding maturity in my life, the lives of my people will be blessed. And I will show my people a way to navigate the selfish, angry, life-robbing speech of the world, speaking back to it not with similar defensive words but with words that bear the hope of the in-breaking kingdom of God in the world. I want to be, by the grace of God, a pastor whose speech is life-giving, redemptive, and rises from the peace of Christ offered to the church (John 20:19).

This renewal of mind that is holiness is a critical component of our mission in and for a world that has become so entirely captivated by a mind-set of individual sovereignty, fear, and despair. The movement of true holiness people is never to isolate from the world in self-protective worry but to engage the world in confident hope. It is hope born of the conviction that there is enough power in the death and resurrection of our Lord Jesus truly to transform life—not only the lives of individuals and communities but the very creation itself (Rom. 8:18-23).

A seminal biblical expression of holiness is the command of God to the people of God given in Leviticus 19:2: "Be holy because I, the Lord your God, am holy." This theme runs throughout Scripture, including a direct quote in Peter's first letter that is joined to the admonition, "Just as he who called you is holy, so be holy in all you do" (1 Pet. 1:15). The way to do this, according to Peter, is through *thinking holy*: a clear focus on the fact that in Christ we are "redeemed from the empty way of life handed down" (v. 18) and that by grace we enjoy the reality of the new birth (v. 23) that enables us to be people of faith, hope, and love (vv. 21-22). These ideas remind me of the oft-quoted verses in Paul's first letter to the Corinthians where the apostle admonishes a congregation too often squeezed into the world's mold to shape it's life together not by power or violence but by love:

> Love is patient, love is kind. It does not envy, it does not boast, it is not proud. It does not dishonor others, it is not self-seeking, it is not easily angered, it keeps no record of wrongs. Love does not delight in evil but rejoices with the truth. It always protects, always trusts, always hopes, always perseveres. Love never fails. (13:4-8)

I have often thought that one could easily replace the word "love" in those verses with the word "holiness" and not diminish anything. *Holiness is patient, holiness is kind . . . holiness is not self-seeking . . . holiness is not easily angered . . .* For these characteristics actually to become operational in the life of any Christian and especially in the life of a pastor, it requires thinking differently than the world tempts and encourages us to think. The manner of life being described by Paul requires thinking holy, which is a gift of grace and a discipline constantly empowered by the Spirit. When pastors think holy, they know that they do not have to hurry or rush, for this kind of love has eternity on its side. When pastors think holy, then kindness is always on the lookout for ways to offer affirmation and appreciation with no worry about one's own diminishment. When pastors think holy, then they can repent from territorial jealousies and put away the threats of perceived cliques and special friendships. When pastors think holy, they would do about anything to avoid making another feel inferior, stupid, or worthless. When pastors think holy, they can surrender the impulse to insist on their own way, giving up the need to hold a grudge or resentment. Pastors who think holy celebrate the growth of another, would do anything to protect the reputation of another, and practice the discipline of halting gossip. Pastors who think holy always trust, always hope, never give up, and never quit under the Spirit-enabled ability to see that our life together is long-term work.

The apostle then says, "Now these three remain: faith, hope and love. But the greatest of these is love" (1 Cor. 13:13). Our pastoral ministries are and should be all about announcing, inspiring, and calling out "faith, hope and love." Each of these connects to holiness. Faith speaks of grace-enabled trust in God's provision for our complete redemption. Hope speaks of the gospel of transformation, which is not only about the salvation of persons but also about the salvation of the whole world. Love speaks of the very essence of holiness, the perfect love of God being shed abroad in our hearts and in our life together. Keeping track (thinking) of these profound and transformational ideas about what holiness really means and about what God in Christ is actually doing in the world through the power and presence of the Holy Spirit helps us to remember that being a pastor places us on the front line of "the ministry of reconciliation" (2 Cor. 5:18) as "Christ's ambassadors, as though God were making his appeal through us" (v. 20). I pray that my colleagues in pastoral ministry, especially you who are early in your long obedience of vocational ministry, will give yourselves above all things to "pursue holiness of heart and life in the fear of the Lord."[4]

Part 2

GOOD LISTENING AND BEING: WESLEYAN PASTORAL PRACTICE

9
LISTENING TO GOD

The role of every pastor is to help keep the church attentive to God. Many have noted this, but one experience in my ministry really drove it home personally. A few years ago, as a new superintendent, I found myself working with a large church seeking to call a new pastor. The church board was composed of highly capable and strong leaders. I quickly realized that they did not really need me to encourage their business culture impulses in vetting candidates and conducting interviews. What they did need someone to do, however, was to keep them attentive to God in the whole process. When they were tempted to trust their own ability, they needed someone to call them to prayers of surrender to the lordship of Jesus Christ. When they were tempted to become discouraged, someone needed to name God's faithful presence and direction, especially when the signs could suggest failure. This is the role of a pastor, and the only way to do it faithfully and do it well is if the pastor is listening to God. Pastors must listen to God so carefully and regularly that they are able to imagine an alternative reality to the one offered by the world.

The ability to listen to God in such a way that one's pastoral leadership is shaped by the hearing suggests practices that create the space to hear. Perhaps this seems obvious, but I can testify from personal experience and from observation of pastors across thirty years that these disciplines are too easily cast aside in the midst of cultures that value busy productivity. I believe in working hard and in being productive. I believe it is important for pastors to provide strong leadership for congregations that secures the life of the people through wise administration. The thing is, unless these practices rise directly from prayerful reflection, they are nothing more than the capacities of any good organizational leader. Pastors are called to more than good organizational leadership. They are called to name God in the midst of congregational worship and life. Too many pastors attempt this work from their foundation of learning and training, which must be included, but it requires much more. Doing the work of naming God in the lives of our people requires sufficient time for solitude from the noises around us so that we can begin to hear God in ways that only those familiar with desert places can fully understand.

Hearing by Keeping Sabbath

Eugene Peterson helped me learn this particularly through his insistence that one of the best things pastors can do for their people is to keep Sabbath. To mention Sabbath in this way is to name a discipline of regular and sustained periods away from the normal pursuits of life. It is about embracing that which renews and restores and avoiding that which depletes and drains. On a weekly basis it means a full day when we stop to rest, renew, and revision. It can also mean other times for special retreats including occasional sabbatical periods of extended rest and renewal.

Pastors have generally been chief among Sabbath breakers, somehow justifying their unrelenting activity from notions of the sheer importance of their work. Thousands upon thousands of burned-out pastors testify that the rationalizations simply do not fly. This is true not only from the standpoint of physical and emotional health but also and especially from the standpoint of spiritual depth. One simply cannot represent the ministry of Christ in congregation and community unless the ministry rises from deep and sustained times of Spirit-directed meditation. This is why Sabbath keeping is so important as the essential listening space for all Christians and perhaps especially so for pastors.

Keeping Sabbath is much more than taking a "day off," which is a concept borrowed again from the culture of commerce. I do believe it is vitally important for pastors to observe a full day away from the tasks of vocational ministry. Doing this, however, does not necessarily translate to authentic Sabbath keeping. The space that is required for Sabbath is space that is created not only by time and location but also by the work of the Spirit, who faithfully draws the people of God into life-giving rhythms of grace. It is God breathing God's people into (inhale) the whole life and love of Trinity and then breathing out (exhale) the people of God as renewed, restored, and ready servants of the kingdom. Knowing this kind of relationship with God requires that which is increasingly rare in our world: silence, solitude, and peace.

Listening through Scripture

Listening to God also applies to pastors as hearers of Scripture. Several components of this are worth noting. First, pastors must be immersed in Scripture devotionally. This is true for every Christian, but it needs particular mention when talking to pastors because they so often approach the Bible to prepare for preaching and teaching. Bible study that happens in preparation for these tasks can and should be devotional. A key part of being able to preach is to allow the text, under the power of the Spirit, to do its work first on the preacher. It's not that this kind of Bible reading is somehow disqualified from personal devotions. However, in addition to Scripture study for teaching, pastors must guard times for the leisurely, careful, openhearted, and prayerful reading of the Bible that is core to personal spiritual growth. Here, listening to God is not so much about discerning the meaning of a text (although this is never dismissed) as it is about entering into the life-giving love of God for the world that is foundational to every Bible text. Thinking of listening to God in this way brings to mind the words of our Lord when speaking of the shepherd: "His sheep follow him because they know his voice" (John 10:4). Listening to God in this way is not only about *mind* but especially about *heart*, learning to detect the voice of our Lord and to distinguish the voice of the Spirit from the myriad voices that bombard us daily.

Another way to listen to God in the hearing of Scripture is through the pastoral work of biblical scholarship. This is simply to say that in the work of Bible exegesis and hermeneutics the pastor not only is

97

conducting a task in order to preach and teach with accuracy and clarity but also so that, when the opportunities for preaching and teaching arise, the pastor is able to stand confidently under the authority of the Spirit and declare, "Thus says the Lord." Consequently, it is absolutely critical that pastors give their congregations the benefit and blessing of fresh and serious study of the Scriptures. Far too often these days, pastors are tempted to rely on the work of others. This may be especially true because present technologies make the work of others so accessible. Certainly a pastor should draw help from the work of those with special skill and training in the reading and interpreting of Scripture. There is certainly nothing wrong with this. The problem comes when the work of others is simply parroted and passed off as if the pastor had actually engaged the text in a personal way. A practical and helpful piece of advice given to me many years ago was to avoid the temptation to go to the commentaries too soon. Exercising this discipline taught me to listen more deeply to Scripture than I was doing while simply relying on the listening of others.

The voice of the community of faith is a critical component of listening to God through the hearing of Scripture. I have in mind here the means of grace that is the church and how the church has heard and taught Scripture through the centuries. This is a balancing word to the idea of personal devotions. I do believe it is critical for all Christians to be personally engaged in Bible reading and study. However, this never should be done privately. In fact, it really never is done privately because the church through many centuries of hearing Scripture is, in a sense, looking over our shoulder every time we sit down to read the Bible meditatively. This is important in many ways, including as a safeguard to privately conceived interpretations that could become heretical teaching. Therefore, to hear Scripture faithfully is to include the hearing of those who have gone before, particularly the voices of those whom the Spirit has anointed for the oversight of the church. The teachings of the church fathers on Scripture are important companions in the faithful hearing of the text. One example of a fine pastoral resource for this work is the *Ancient Christian Commentary on Scripture* series with Thomas Oden as general editor.[1] Reading the fathers reminds one that Scripture was not really viewed by our forebears as a tool for private study or merely academic interest. In order for Scripture to be read and heard faithfully it must never be isolated from the worshipping community. Therefore, this communal hearing of Scripture remains a central activity of the people of God, gathered by the Spirit to hear the Word of the Lord and to receive the gift of Communion, forming us as the church—the people of God in Christ.

Time and Space for Listening

A very practical piece of this essential work of listening to God is that pastors should take care to order their schedules and work spaces so that they can daily place first things first. Many pastors find it helpful to guard the first hours of the day for these purposes, making the most of what tend to be the quieter hours of the day. This is a special challenge for the great company of pastors who must work a job in addition to pastoral responsibilities in order to care for their families. This has not been my experience, so I hesitate to offer any advice to you. Gladly, there seems to be increasing focus on so-called bivocational pastors and greater resources to assist them. No doubt, it becomes important for these pastors to talk to one another about the practical task of managing schedule and energy.

One strategy that may be helpful to all pastors is one I was taught many years ago. Eugene Peterson said that the trick to really protecting time for listening is to get one's calendar before anyone else does, literally marking out the times for prayer and the study of Scripture. One friend of mine used to place on his calendar one- or two-hour appointments with people like the apostle Paul, Augustine, John Wesley, or Karl Barth. He found it useful when someone was asking for time to be able to say, "Sorry, I already have an appointment scheduled for that time." Whatever the strategy, it takes intention and planning for any pastor to protect space for these essential activities. The irony is that no one really gets after us if we don't do this. Typically, if folks become upset with our work it is because we are not meeting their needs or desires in a time that suits them. This is not to suggest that responding to the needs of our people is unimportant, but we simply cannot allow a sort of constant emergency response mind-set to overtake the deliberate protection of time and space for study.

Using the word "study" above brings up one more point in this discussion that I hope is more than my own hobbyhorse. Within my lifetime it seems we moved from the pastor's *study* to the pastor's *office*. Of course, I am referring to the physical space reserved for the pastor's ministry tools (library, desk, computer, counseling chairs, and so forth). I think this is a subtle indication of how the whole idea of pastor has been captivated by business leadership ideas. In light of the focus of this chapter, I would challenge any pastor who has a sign on the door reading "pastor's office" to change it on purpose back to "pastor's study." Perhaps this would say something to you and to your people about what it really means for you to be the pastor: one who remembers that your first work is to keep the congregation attentive to God as one who is carefully listening to God.

10
LISTENING TO PEOPLE

The core pastoral task of listening well to people was discussed in chapter 6 under the conversation about spiritual direction. The present discussion intends to turn toward some of the practical components of being a good listener. The following practices and strategies are all predicated upon the core pastoral qualities that have come into view up to this point in the book. Even if one completely affirms the importance of pastors being good listeners, this fact does not in itself make one a good listener. It is quite easy for pastors to become distracted by so many needs and tasks that they do not listen well. My role as superintendent regularly places me with church boards and pastors to conduct a review of congregational health. The relationship of pastor-congregation is a vital component of the review. One area for growth that is often identified by laypeople for their pastor is the capacity to communicate that they really do listen. Active listening is a learned skill and can be developed through discipline and practice.

Unhurried

Pastoral ministry is complex in the number of distinct activities and responsibilities that compose the work. There is a wonderful rhythm to pastoral work that moves toward and then from the climax of Lord's Day worship. The hundreds of tasks that must be completed within this rhythm often mean that pastors are thought of and referred to as "busy people." Henri Nouwen noted that in our time the idea of *busy* has become something like a badge of honor, as if "busy" and "important" mean the same thing.[1] Pastors are not immune to the temptation to enjoy being thought of by their people as busy. It plays right in to their need to be considered either important or at least a worthwhile financial investment by the people who give to pay their salaries. I suppose I would like to be thought of as busy rather than lazy. However, there is something about my people thinking of me as "so busy" that perhaps should bother me. What am I communicating to them about my ability and willingness to listen to them and to know them in ways that express not only my care but also God's care?

My practice of pastoral care, especially the practice of listening, has been profoundly shaped by Eugene Peterson's idea that pastors should have the capacity "to be unhurried with another person."[2] This phrase literally becomes a mental cue as I sit with people in my study to listen, counsel, and pray with them. Usually these conversations come in the midst of many other tasks and activities, and I often find myself sitting there watching the person talk but not really listening because I am mentally reviewing my "to do" list. Reminding myself that listening well is an essential component of my work really does help me put away those distractions and focus fully and prayerfully on what the individual is sharing. I inwardly rehearse the phrase, "unhurried with another person." Exercising this kind of discipline in pastoral conversations opens space for prayer, even while listening to the other. My experience and the testimony of other pastors is that when we enter those moments as fully present spiritual directors, the Spirit gives us gifts of discernment and even of speech. On more than one occasion as I sat with someone pouring out a problem, I thought to myself, "I have no idea what to say about this." And yet, as I remained prayerful and attentive, thoughts came that turned to speech. Regularly, after responding to someone under my counsel, I sat back and thought to myself, "That was a great answer, but I know I did not come up with that on my own. Thank you, Lord."

Active Listening

Active listening includes not only what we do with our ears but also what we do with our eyes, our mouths, and even our posture. My wife and I have learned that to communicate well we must give attention to these attendant dynamics of good listening. Consequently, we do not usually attempt to have important conversations while driving in the car or while lying in bed in the darkness, staring at the ceiling (that would be *me* staring, *her* talking). We have productive conversation when sitting face-to-face, sometimes holding hands, and always looking directly at one another, having eliminated common noises like television or smartphones. I recognize that an awful lot of conversation happens in the midst of life noises, but the most important conversations deserve careful attention to guarding the space for active listening.

Similarly, important pastoral conversations are assisted by giving attention to the physical location and the setting of these conversations. Sitting at a low, round table rather than across a big desk, or sitting in chairs clearly designed more for leisure than for business—a simple posture communicates something to a parishioner about the pastor's openness to authentic conversation. Making eye contact and acknowledging the other's speech with affirming nods, verbal cues of recognition, and appropriately timed responses are the kinds of practical tools that pastors should learn and develop to be good listeners.

Reflective listening suggests that we discipline ourselves to avoid rushing to give advice or to share our own perspective. We must begin instead by making sure that the communication is clear through the practice of reflecting back to the speaker what we have heard. This serves two purposes. First, it lets the speaker know we are truly listening. Second, it helps to avoid misunderstanding by giving the speaker a chance either to confirm or correct what we have heard. This can seem a bit awkward at first if one is not accustomed to doing it, but with practice it becomes natural to respond with, "What I am hearing you say is . . ." or "Let me make sure I am understanding you . . ." These practices may be especially important when the conversation begins with angry words of accusation or blame. Our impulse may be to answer the accusation or to defend ourselves from faulty assumptions. Rushing to answer or defend only serves to build barriers to effective communication. The strong emotions that can easily attend difficult conversations should not be ignored. They are best addressed up front through acknowledgment and then through seeking clarity of what really is at issue. This is especially important when the conversation is seeking to address a conflict between the conversation partners. The negative emotions of the difference must be dealt with first before we can clear the way actually to negotiate the difference (more on this in chapter 15).

Putting Away Busy

Pastors may need to become proactive in correcting the language of parishioners about their "busyness." Ever had someone say, "Oh, Pastor, I hate to bother you, I know you are so busy"? Maybe the first thing we should do there is to correct the assumption. Doing so would mean that we have become secure and confident in our sense of priorities and our value to the congregation. Perhaps our response to that kind of opening should be something such as, "Yes, I do have a full schedule, but I am not so busy that I cannot listen to you." Responding in this way could serve at least two important purposes: it affirms the worth of the person approaching us, and it corrects the notion that *busy* means *unavailable*. I have consistently instructed staff members to remember that the unexpected interruptions that come into our days are, in fact, an important part of our work. Let me hasten to add here that boundaries are crucial. Communicating availability does not mean that I rush about nervously trying to meet everyone's need. It is possible to communicate and offer genuine availability and access without casting aside one's priorities of calling and mission. Especially important here is the point made by Dan Spaite, when he suggests that most pastors need a new definition of crisis.[3] Just because someone claims to be in crisis does not necessarily mean that we must drop everything and rush to the person's side. There are certainly important times when this must be done, but there are other times when what is being reported as crisis has actually been taking place for some time. It may simply be an acute point in an otherwise chronic dysfunction that may in fact need our ministry but probably can wait for our planned availability.

Another way to re-image the idea of being busy is to give special attention to how we pastors manage "foyer conversations." I am thinking about those important moments and informal encounters that happen before and after services and during other gatherings when we engage in dozens of serial, conversational exchanges. One of the real challenges here is to be fully present to the person before us when, out of the corner of our eye, we see another person waiting to talk to us. This moment is especially perilous if we would really rather engage the person waiting than the person who now has our ear. I learned from one of my mentors the importance of giving the person before me my full attention, primarily through eye contact, rather than constantly looking at the people waiting to speak to me. The lesson came when I heard congregation members talk about how much they appreciated this pastor's full attention to them in conversation and how it communicated a sense of his care and their value. If we give way to distractions in interpersonal communication, it says to the person trying to speak to us that he or she is not nearly as important as the person who is next in line. This does not mean that we allow the person to monopolize our time in this situation. Something we have to learn is what my mentor playfully called "terminal facility," meaning the capacity to end a conversation in a grace-giving and affirming way. But listening to people in ways that reflect the care and concern of our Lord for the people is essential pastoral work.

Group Listening

Another arena of important pastoral listening is that which happens within groups. I am thinking here especially of the pastor's role in leading meetings, perhaps board meetings or committee meetings. One of the common frustrations that I hear being expressed by members of church boards is that the pastor does not really listen. Sometimes this simply means that the pastor will not give way to every demanding expectation of a particular member. But there are other times when the pastor really has not learned to listen well as a group leader. Much of current leadership discussion seems to cast the vision of a confidant, articulate leader so full of vision and passion that once the pastor speaks his or her profound insights, the conversation ends and everyone gets in line. It is certainly true that in most leadership contexts there do come moments when decisive and strong leadership is necessary. Most of the time, however, the capacity to exercise this kind of leadership is built through careful listening that serves to build the critical components of trust and confidence.

A leader who listens well in groups has learned the skills of posture that communicate engagement. For example, rather than sitting back with arms folded, fiddling with paperwork, or staring at a screen, a good group listener communicates patience as the other is working to articulate his or her point of view. Therefore, a good listener does not cut off the speaker when he or she is struggling to find the right words. A good listener signals care through eye contact, acknowledging nods, or verbal cues of receptivity. Sometimes taking notes on what the speaker is saying can communicate careful listening. This kind of listening requires much discipline because it is so easy to jump to respond in ways that actually communicate a lack of authentic engagement. A good listening leader also needs to guard against answering with so many words that the sheer weight of the response dampens open and authentic dialogue.

The Cost of Listening

There is one more component of pastoral listening that I want to offer as a word of caution and preparation to my young colleagues in ministry. I was perhaps fifteen years into the work of vocational ministry when it really hit me that I had not been prepared for the personal cost of receiving the confessions of my people. I did not notice so much at first, but over time the weight of hearing the sinful brokenness of my people as they confessed their sins to their pastor began to take its toll on me. To this day, there are things I have heard that I really wish I had never heard. There are things I was caused to imagine through these confessions that I wish I had never been caused to imagine. I have been able to share some things with my wife or a close and trusted colleague as a way to deal with the emotional toll. Some of the most difficult things, however, I will take with me to my grave. (Exceptions would be when one confesses harm to a child or plans for self-harm, for example.) This is part of the cost of serving as a pastor. We are not helpless in this regard, however. Certainly, this is part of why significant times for daily prayer and reflection are critical. The Spirit who is our Comforter and Guide is the primary resource we have for handling the painful side of listening. We should also occasionally access the skill of professional counselors who are gifted and trained to help us sort out the thoughts and emotions that can become damaging to the soul if left unattended. No pastor should ever feel ashamed to turn to a therapist or counselor as part of tending to intrapersonal health. This is part of why the fellowship of pastors is so important and so wonderful. It is good to be with people who know what it means to be a pastor. Even without the exchange of particular stories, the general acknowledgment of this cost by one who knows it personally is in itself an encouragement. It is another way in which pastors can do the work of God through listening.

11
BEING PREACHER

Most pastors seem to locate preaching somewhere near the center of their work. Many pastors testify that the work of preaching is what they enjoy most about pastoral ministry. In fairness, not all pastors feel this way. Some see it as a huge and relentless burden from which they will never find relief. Either way, preaching is one of the significant pastoral acts in the communion of God's people. Thinking about the act of preaching, it may seem counterintuitive in our time that people would find value in sitting before a "talking head" for thirty minutes or more. Some preachers, recognizing this, have tried any number of strategies to be more image based, more conversational, and create a greater sense of congregational participation in the sermon. These may be fine strategies, and sometimes they are employed with great effect. However, there is one inescapable fact that must be embraced by anyone who accepts the call of God to preach the Word. It is that God has chosen and continues to choose preaching as a central component of evangelism and mission. Paul wrote to the Corinthians,

> For since in the wisdom of God the world through its wisdom did not know him, God was pleased through the foolishness of what was preached to save those who believe. Jews demand signs and Greeks look for wisdom, but we preach Christ crucified. (1 Cor. 1:21-23)

We preach because God blesses faithful preaching. We preach because we continue to recognize the presence of the Holy Spirit in the reading, hearing, study, and proclamation of the Scriptures, pointing all in our hearing to God's reconciling work through Jesus Christ.

I have always worked in pastoral ministry from the conviction not only that people need the work of a faithful preacher but also that God's people are hungry for biblical preaching. This conviction has only been deepened in my present work, which places me in a different congregation each Sunday. In some places, the people are clearly being blessed by the skillful and anointed work of the preacher. The Spirit uses strong and biblical preaching to help God's people "grow up" in Christ (Eph. 4). This is a beautiful thing when it happens, and anyone who is able to discern these things can see quickly when a congregation is well loved through the work of pastoral preaching. Unfortunately, it also becomes painfully evident when this is missing. Where strong, biblical preaching is not happening, the sheep are scrawny and agitated and the health of the congregation is diminished. This is often the case even among people who are mature and disciplined enough to practice spiritual formation in their own lives. Nothing fully replaces the power of Spirit-anointed, biblically based, and lovingly delivered preaching.

Several years ago this truth hit me in a fresh way. I was on vacation and visiting a sister congregation in another state. I enjoyed every aspect of the service, but I was especially looking forward to the sermon. I think it has to do with the same way my wife enjoys a meal when she didn't have to prepare it. The pastor took his text from Romans 8 that day, the latter part where Paul makes that glorious declaration of our security in God's love. The sermon was very well done and delivered with the obvious love of a pastor's heart. As I listened and participated by the Spirit, I realized something about the nature of preaching. All through the sermon, I could fairly predict what the conclusion was going to be. I had preached that text many times, and I could just imagine how the pastor would probably bring the sermon to its climactic point. My fresh discovery, however, was that even though I knew what was going to be proclaimed, I really *wanted* him to say it! I couldn't wait for him to say it. I didn't know exactly what words or phrases he might use, but I became excited about hearing the pastor say what he did indeed ultimately declare, that in Christ we are no longer doomed to a life of constant struggle and doubt. *Preach it, brother!* No matter what life may dish out on us, we are "more than conquerors through him who loved us" (v. 37). *Praise God!*

I left the service that day with a new perspective on how my people came to Sunday service. I realized that on any given Sunday there were many people before me who did not know what the message of Romans 8 would be. However, there were many others who walked the way of Jesus long enough to be able to predict the point of the message on almost any text. Does that mean it was not as meaningful to them? No, they still needed to hear the good news proclaimed just as much as those who were new seekers.

I wonder if we pastors are too often tricked into thinking that our sermons have to be cleverly innovative and "new" in order to gain a hearing. I am certainly an advocate of excellence and imaginative creativity in preaching. On that day, however, I was reminded that nothing is as powerful as the straightforward and clear proclamation of the simple good news that "if God is for us, who can be against us?" (v. 31). Pre-Christian persons need to hear it. New believers need to hear it. Old saints need to hear it. And pastors even need to hear it.

Biblical Preaching

To speak of biblical preaching is not to focus on a particular method. Sound biblical preaching can be expositional, narrative, topical, inductive, or deductive. These choices are not incidental in effectively communicating the Word of God, but nearly any homiletical approach may or may not be biblical preaching. Biblical preaching happens as a work of the Holy Spirit, who inspires the preacher in prayerful study of the text and then in the crafting, delivery, and hearing of the sermon in ways that inspire the response of God's people to the inspired Word of God. Folks can walk away from a sermon saying, "That was a great speech." This kind of response may gratify the preacher, but every pastor would much rather hear someone say, "I need to do this (whatever *this* may be) in response to hearing God's Word today." When biblical preaching happens, the focus is not on the preacher at all but on the power of the Spirit working through the text and the preacher to speak a fresh word to the gathered community of faith.

Having lived and worked near my denominational seminary for many years, I have been blessed to preach in the seminary chapel on several occasions. That can be a daunting prospect as one looks over the chapel congregation to see highly skilled scholars about to sit under one's ministry of preaching. (Actually, I learned early that scholars in Bible, theology, and ministry need a pastor just as much as anyone else.) One day after preaching in the seminary chapel, one of our most revered scholars made his way directly toward me. My first thought was, "Oh no, what did I say that was wrong?" He actually said to me, "When you preach, I appreciate that you are careful with the Scriptures." It could be that this was simply the most charitable thing he could think of to say. I took it as more than that. I received his words and continue to receive his words as a challenge that the preacher must take care never to get in the way of the text or of what the Spirit wants to do through the text in the lives of the people of God.

Several things potentially could get in the way of care for the Scriptures. One of them is the contemporary desire to be *contemporary*, which I think often means something like casual, familiar, or entertaining. The potential problem here is when attention to the form displaces attention to the substance. Again, form is not incidental, but it cannot bear the weight alone of that which is our task in biblical preaching. Too often it seems that preachers are working a lot harder on their PowerPoint slides than they are on what they actually wanted to say as a result of their study. I know that pastors sometimes spend hours finding just the right movie clip to show, when they might do well to spend as much time on study of the text or in prayer. This suggests another potential barrier to good biblical preaching, which is failing to guard the time and space for the work of study and reflection that good preaching requires.

Pastors sometimes joke about the "Saturday night special." In my opinion, this is no joke and could represent a colossal failure on the part of the pastor. It may happen occasionally that the work of ministry in any given week squeezes out the times for prayer, study, and preparation of the sermon. This is understandable and in these circumstances preachers must do their very best in light of the limited opportunity for preparation. However, if this becomes a pattern in one's ministry, it begins to reveal a fatal flaw in one's pastoral theology when it comes to prioritizing the work of ministry. This is a point at which I believe today's pastors need to be ruthlessly honest about what actually occupies their time. So much time can be squandered in idle conversation, secondary tasks that feel more comfortable, or following the relentless lure of entertainments through various media. To the degree that any of us struggle to discipline our time, we need corresponding accountability systems to help us in "making the most of every opportunity" (Eph. 5:16).

I do not write this without thinking again about my pastoral colleagues who are in so-called bivocational ministries. Some pastors are working full-time jobs to take care of their families and are having to figure out how to do the necessary study and preparation for leading worship, not to mention all the other pastoral duties. I can imagine that these pastors rely on the helps provided by other pastors who have more time to do this work. I see absolutely nothing wrong with doing this so long as it is done honestly and carefully. By *honestly* I mean, give credit where credit is due. This does not mean you need to fill the sermon with constant verbal footnotes, but when you are using large portions of another's work, that fact should be noted in some simple way. By *carefully* I mean, enter prayerfully and passionately into the process of choosing the helps and doing more than just reading them out on Sunday. Take them into your heart. Work with the ideas and make the language your own. If you are unable to take another's work into your heart so that the preaching is passionate and personal, this is a sure sign that you have not chosen the help well. Lately it seems there has been much focus on plagiarism, particularly in academia. This focus is appropriate and needed, but it should not scare preachers away from using good tools provided by others to help us all become better preachers. As one who was blessed with time to do this work and who published sermon helps in the past, I am pleased to know that I may be able to help bivocational colleagues in this way.[1] So, I am trying to say to these friends that there is no shame here so long as you do not become slothful or dishonest in the use of another's work.

One of my favorite descriptions of preaching came from Dr. Tom Long, who suggested that we might understand pastoral preaching as the pastor going to the text in service to the congregation, hoping to make a discovery. Then the preacher announces that discovery to the congregation. Or, even better, the preacher takes the congregation on the journey of the discovery. I like this description because to me it images a pastor engaged lovingly in the work of exegesis and homiletics. Pastors do not approach the work of sermonizing just to check something off the "to do" list. Nor do good pastors approach the task selfishly, caring more about their own discoveries or their skillful delivery than about the condition and response of the hearers. Careful pastors work at preaching *in service to the congregation* as an act of love. This way of describing the task also reminds that much of the work of preparing to preach is done under the surface, in the closet, where no one but the Father sees. In other words, so much of preparing to preach well is to pray well.

Gordon Lathrop, following the work of Yngve Brilioth, draws from the Lukan text of Jesus preaching in the synagogue at Nazareth (4:14-30) to suggest this as a seminal model of Christian preaching.[2] Particularly he notes the sermon takes place within the context of worship (a *liturgical* event), that it rises from a Scripture text (an *exegetical* event), and that it speaks into the present (a *prophetic* event). Lathrop works from here to suggest that all Christian preaching should be liturgical, exegetical, and prophetic. By *liturgical* he simply means to say that the location of preaching is not incidental. Christian preaching lives in the midst of the gathered people of God for worship, as the congregation praises, prays, hears the Word, is gathered to the Table, and sent on mission into the world. This location matters deeply in order for preaching to be anything more than a great speech. It must be the Spirit-inspired interpretation of the sacred texts that are read in the assembly, so that the people of God under the authority of their pastor have a chance to respond in faith to the Word of the Lord. By *exegetical* Lathrop means that preaching rises not from the capricious selection of text by the preacher but by coming under the authority of the text that is given to the church and preaching *from* the text, not using the text to support one's own agenda. Even Jesus, Lathrop notes, was *handed* the scroll of Isaiah in the Luke 4 account. While most Christian congregations are accustomed to working with assigned texts (lectionary), others are just learning the power and value of subjugating the will of preacher and congregation to the will of the larger body of Christ in the selection of texts for Christian worship and preaching. By *prophetic*, then, Gordon Lathrop is talking about the purpose of preaching as calling out faith. It should be eschatological in that it casts a vision of the in-breaking kingdom of God inaugurated in the life, death, and resurrection of our Lord. The Luke 4 sermon of Jesus culminates in the hope-filled proclamation, "Today this scripture is fulfilled in your hearing" (v. 21). Similarly, faithful biblical preaching must always announce good news that not only inspires hope but also calls forth an obedient life response.

One of my favorite ways to think about the work of pastoral preaching is to think of creating a congregational conversation over time. This is one of the things I miss the most in my current work of itinerant ministry. I think there is nothing better than walking with a congregation through a text over time and witnessing how the hearing and study of that text begins to work its way into the language and conversations of a people. Preaching through books of the Bible can lend itself to this kind of outcome. Topical preaching can do this as well, so long as care is taken to plan the scope and sequence of the series carefully. One must also choose Bible texts carefully in this kind of preaching to avoid the less than desirable approach of simply finding a verse or two that loosely connects with what I really want to say. This is not biblical preaching. There are at least two key ways to preaching biblically. One is to begin with the text, either chosen or assigned by the church, and go wherever faithful study of the text leads. The other is to take a problem or need to the text and discover how Scripture speaks to the issue. In either approach, I find that the very best way to connect a congregation to the story of God through the Scriptures is to do careful annual planning. My friend David Busic has written a helpful chapter on this in *The Pastor's Guide to Effective Preaching*, so I will not go deeply into the process here.[3] However, there are four key questions that pastors should have in mind when planning the preaching calendar.

Planning to Preach

First is the question of where we find ourselves on any given Sunday in the Christian calendar. The church marks time differently than the world does. Our concern is not so much the lunar or civil calendar as it is the annual rehearsing of the story of redemption in the birth, life, passion, death, and resurrection of our Lord—his ascension and the outpouring of the Spirit on Pentecost. The telling of this story across twenty-six weeks can be done not only by following the particular texts given to us by the church for these days (i.e., lectionary) but also by noting the themes on which each of these seasons of the Christian year calls us to focus. For example, Epiphany is a particular day in the Christian year but launches a period of several weeks prior to Lent where the church focuses on the revelation of Jesus as the Christ. This basic theme can connect in so many ways, from Bible texts that focus on this truth to the concerns and issues being faced by our people in their everyday lives. So the first question for planning a preaching calendar is, "What is the church saying to us on this particular Sunday about the story of God?"

The second question for planning a preaching calendar is, "How can we ensure our people are hearing from a balance of the various literary forms of the Bible?" Our Scriptures contain history, prophetic speech, wisdom, gospel, letters, and apocalyptic, and there are forms within these forms, such as narrative, poetry, exhortation, and many others. Each of us has his or her favorite kinds of texts and areas of greatest comfort for preaching. However, it is important for our people to hear preaching from a balance of texts, which is something that lectionaries provide for us. Whether or not a preacher follows a lectionary weekly, regularly consulting one can help with this balance.[4]

A third important question for planning a preaching calendar concerns the pastoral work of discerning the present needs of the congregation: "What are the concerns and issues that the people are facing in their families, workplaces, and personal lives?" Much of this information is discovered from the mining of pastoral conversations over time or even from inviting the people to offer their questions and concerns as the pastor prepares to enter this planning time. My pastoral practice was to announce to the congregation each year that I would be going away for one week for the sole purpose of planning prayerfully the preaching calendar. A few weeks ahead of that time, I would invite the congregation to respond by completing statements or questions, such as,

- The thing I really do not understand about the Christian way is . . .
- What does our church believe about . . . ?
- My biggest spiritual struggle is . . .
- Please pray for me about . . .

Taking these responses with me into the planning week, I would spend the first day doing nothing other than going over the things that my people were sharing, and praying for them, asking God to help me as their pastor to love them and help them through the work of carefully preaching the texts of Scripture. Working with this question alone creates more preaching ideas and opportunities than a pastor can address in several years.

The fourth question for planning a preaching calendar is to ask, "What does the congregation need to hear concerning mission?" This is about making sure our preaching does not focus only on helping people in their personal lives and individual discipleship. This is about focusing on our life together and what it means for us as a community of faith to engage and participate in God's mission in the world.

Preaching is a vast subject that is worthy of constant study and discipline. Growing preachers are constantly learning from others how to preach better. Good preachers listen to good preaching. Good preachers read good sermons. Most of all, good preachers are compelled by love for God and love for God's people not only to "rightly [divide] the word of truth" (2 Tim. 2:15, KJV) but also to proclaim it effectively through imaginative and inspiring speech. In these ways, the work of preaching is one of the most beautiful acts of a pastor seeking to love his or her congregation well.

12
BEING EVANGELIST

The charge that is given to those being ordained in my ecclesial connection is drawn largely from the text of 2 Timothy 4:1-5 and includes this specific charge: "Do the work of an evangelist" (v. 5). I wonder what the people, including those who are being ordained, imagine when they hear these words? What exactly is the work of an evangelist? How do we know whether or not the work of evangelism is being done?

The congregation that raised me gave a simple and clear understanding of what this means: it was about leading someone through conversation to pray the sinner's prayer. I grew up being mightily impressed with those who seemed to know how to "get people saved." Often these folks were my pastors, but sometimes I heard testimonies of other Christians who not only were successful in bearing witness to the saving grace of God in Christ but who also seemed especially to enjoy telling about "closing the deal," complete with many tears and shouts of joy. I figured at an early age that our pastor's main job was to lead people to Jesus. This idea was only reinforced when I saw one of Wesley's twelve rules for preachers prominently displayed on the wall behind the pastor's desk, "You have nothing to do but to save souls."[1] I am not about to argue that this understanding of a pastor's work is somehow misguided. However, I do think we need to attend to some of the implications and perhaps even misunderstandings that can become attached to this way of thinking about the work of evangelism.

One of these implications, or perhaps unintended outcomes, is that evangelism comes to be viewed as a fairly private transaction. Our mission, in this view, is to get everyone we can to make a decision for Jesus, to pray the sinner's prayer, and be added to the number of those who were saved this year. In fact, we *should* be able to name the names of those who, under the influence of our community of faith, have come to know God's love for them in Christ and have entered into the life of the church through the sacrament of baptism. For those who were baptized but became distant from the life of the church, this may include their testimony of freshly embraced faith and the reaffirmation of their baptism as the community of faith celebrates with them the grace of God at work in their lives (more on this in chapter 14). Keeping confessions of faith connected to the life of the church, especially the sacrament of baptism, helps us remember that evangelism is about much more than making a decision for Jesus. Evangelism is about the testimony of the church to the world that God's mission of bringing all of creation under the complete rule and reign of Christ has begun and continues, evidenced significantly by the transformed lives of those "who once were far away" but now "have been brought near by the blood of Christ" (Eph. 2:13).

This is why part of leading a congregation well in the area of evangelism must include the pastoral leadership of providing space for testimonies. These testimonies include not only the stories of those who have recently come to confess faith in Christ, though these are essential and necessary to vibrant congregational life, but also the ongoing stories of how God's people are *being converted*, or perhaps more precisely, about sanctification. This is to say something not only about the spiritual journey of individuals but especially about the spiritual journey of a people together. This is actually the meaning of being sanctified "entirely" according to 1 Thessalonians 5:23. Dr. Tom Noble teaches that in the Greek text of this verse, the word translated "entirely" is not an adverb to modify "sanctify" but an adjective to modify "you" (plural), meaning the people of God.[2]

When Christians learn and express that growing into Christlikeness is no private affair, we then can see that evangelism also is not a private affair but a natural part of healthy congregational life. The church is not an incidental collection of folks who have become Christians but the very body of Christ, gathered by the Spirit into the life-giving work of prayer, the active hearing of Scripture, and the glad-hearted reception of grace through bread and wine. (This is why it is such an affront when Christians attach to congregations on the basis of little more than consumer preferences.) In this way of thinking, evangelism is so much more than personal conversations that lead someone to pray a sinner's prayer, although it can and should include this. Evangelism more completely is the work of the whole church as we live together and toward the world in ways that become an authentic reflection of the universal rule and reign of God in Christ. When the church lives and works together faithfully and effectively in furthering God's mission, then people are drawn to the grace that is expressed in the quality, passion, and purpose of our lives individually and especially together. This is holiness.

From this foundational understanding of evangelism, there is specific work for a pastor to do in leading a congregation in evangelism. A present danger at this point is something that I encounter regularly in conversations with local church leaders: laypeople are quick to give this over entirely to the pastor. This betrays a narrow understanding of evangelism as being something like "convincing the unconvinced to follow Jesus." Many Christians are more than happy to defer to the pastor for this kind of intimidating work. To the degree that Wesley's rule ("You have nothing to do but to save souls") does shape the pastoral work of evangelism, how does this become actualized in the weekly rhythm of pastoral life? While the work of what has sometimes been called *personal evangelism* remains important for pastors and laity alike, the pastoral discipline of evangelism has much to do with shaping congregational identity as an authentic expression of the kingdom of God, through which the gospel is proclaimed. So, how does this pastoral shaping take place?

Worship as Evangelism

First, pastors in the contemporary evangelical movement need a fresh understanding that worship *is* evangelism. The gospel is announced when the people of God, gathered by the Spirit, enact their faith in authentic biblical, sacramental, and missional worship. Recent expressions of so-called worship have at times become so captivated by consumer interests of event, spectacle, and attraction that the components of authentic worship get muted beneath a sensory bombardment of sounds and images. Underneath any concerns for form or style, however, are the essential components of Christian worship that, under the blessing of the Holy Spirit, bear witness to the world of the good news that God was in Christ "reconciling the world to himself" (2 Cor. 5:19). The evangelistic power of Christian worship rises from grace, and grace alone. The gospel is proclaimed as the Spirit of our risen Lord moves in and through the gathered community of faith in the hearing of Scripture, the teaching of godly pastors, prayer, Communion, and the sending of the gifts of God (grace and peace) through the people of God into the world.

The evangelistic power of Scripture in the worshipping community cannot be overstated. Unfortunately, too many congregations give barely a nod to the reading and hearing of Scripture in services of worship. As one who visits a different congregation every Sunday, I am sometimes amazed that there could be an entire service, sermon included, without any explicit offering of the Bible. Conversely, I am more often richly blessed, challenged, and edified when careful intention is given to the reading of Scripture lessons. Most Christian congregations, including an increasing number of evangelical churches, follow the direction of the wider church in the reading of the Bible throughout the Christian year. This does not necessarily translate to a so-called liturgical form of worship. Many forms can and should include the prominence of Scripture readings carefully prepared and intentionally executed in ways that draw the congregation, including seekers, into an encounter with the living Word.

Closely related to this is the evangelistic power of the sermon. Some pastors seem to make a false distinction between evangelistic preaching and other kinds of preaching. When evangelism is properly understood as announcing the universal reign of God in Christ, then every sermon should be evangelistic—or it is not a sermon. Preaching from any Bible text and under any theme can only become faithful preaching when the sermon points to Christ and offers the gospel. This being said, it is certainly appropriate and necessary that the pastor's annual preaching calendar would include specific sermons that explicitly call people to confess Jesus Christ as Lord, which happens best when the preaching is connected to what the church has always understood to be the center of Christian worship: the Lord's Supper. We will focus on the pastoral work of setting the Table in chapter 14, but here the Eucharist needs to be connected not only to preaching but especially to evangelism. Well known is Wesley's view that the sacrament of Holy Communion is a "converting ordinance," which is not to suggest that we open the Table to the unbaptized ("the feast is for his disciples"[3]), but that in the faithful worship of the Christian community at the Lord's Supper, the Holy Spirit is present not only to offer grace to the church but also to "convict the world concerning sin" (John 16:8, ESV).

Perhaps one of the most critical components of Christian worship as an occasion of evangelism is the intentional sending forth of the people of God into the world on mission. The pastoral work of benediction can be not only a beautiful work but also a powerfully shaping work as we stand representing Christ to pronounce the blessings of grace and peace upon the people. Benediction broadly understood should also include explicit charge to the church to be evangelists, to go everywhere with Jesus announcing the good news of the kingdom of God. Often the words of the benediction come directly from Scripture, as in the well-known priestly blessing of Numbers 6:24-26: "The LORD bless you and keep you; the LORD make his face shine upon you and be gracious to you; the LORD turn his face toward you and give you peace." Other times the blessing may be from the pastor's own words, such as this blessing I once gave to the congregation having preached from Romans 12: "May the Lord bless you with the ability to love one another. May God give you grace to live as reconcilers. And may we become a testimony to the world of the reconciling love of God in Christ." Our people live in a world filled with hurtful words. They receive messages every day of how inadequate they are. In a world based on competition and marked by violence, our people often come to worship with their Christian identity out of focus and their spiritual esteem damaged. As pastors, we have a great privilege and responsibility to remind them of who they really are in Christ. We can speak words to them that call them to reckon their lives according to the values of the kingdom of God rather than the kingdoms of this world. I understand this as part of the work of an evangelist.

Many forms and styles can faithfully bear these essential components. All forms of a worshipping community should be done with prayerful and careful intention and excellence, but the effectiveness of Christian worship is not in the forms, no matter how impressively done. The evangelistic effect of Christian worship is in the testimony of God's people to the redeeming love of our triune God and the good news of the healing and redemption of all things. This being said, the authentic worship of the community of faith is not the end of the story for evangelism. It is in many ways the beginning and leads to further considerations about the work of evangelism by the church.

Teaching Christians to Bear Witness

From worship then, with no diminishment in importance, is the necessity of pressing the claims of the gospel upon the unsaved, person by person. Having done the first work of worship well certainly does not mean that the church is finished with the work of evangelism, which becomes a critical point for pastoral direction. Doing the work of an evangelist as a pastor certainly includes teaching the people how to take what is being formed in them through Christian worship into the world. This includes several things. One important component is the pastoral work of broadening the vision and perspective of congregants so that they begin not only to realize but also to act on the truth that the whole of their lives bears witness (or not) to Christ. Particularly in the evangelical movement, Christians tend to think of witness only as a specific transaction of sharing one's faith with another. Stories abound of how a believer led someone to Jesus, often while seated together on an airplane! It is certainly important to prepare our people for these inevitable opportunities, but teaching them to bear witness in the world will also include helping them connect their daily decisions to how those decisions may or may not be a faithful witness. For example, in most societies the economic status of an individual or family is evident by observing the choices they make concerning housing, transportation, clothing, activities, and so forth. Teaching whole-life stewardship that helps our people to be countercultural in their values, debt, use of time, service, hospitality, and a whole host of other issues is a major part of shaping the evangelistic bearing of congregations and individual Christians. Even the way we think about the programming of the local congregation becomes a part of this. Does our schedule of activities and programs simply reflect the frenetic pace and consumer orientation of contemporary culture? Or are we faithfully calling out a community that does not exist naturally in the world—one that lives in simplicity, freedom, and peace? This is evangelism just as sure as telling someone how to receive Jesus as his or her Savior.

But this is not an either/or proposition. Teaching evangelism certainly does include showing our people specific ways to prepare to "give the reason for the hope" (1 Pet. 3:15) to everyone who asks. Consequently, a major part of pastoral work is to help people move from fearfulness to confidence when it comes to verbally sharing their faith with the people they encounter day by day. This can happen in multiple ways that may include one-on-one discipleship and mentoring, Christian education in small groups, or even larger group teaching and training that addresses not only how to prepare one's testimony but also how to sharpen one's awareness for those moments of openness that develop in authentic relationship with people who do not yet confess Christ.

As a pastor I did this in multiple ways, including dedicating Sunday evening services to walking the whole group through role-play scenarios of how to share the gospel in everyday conversations. The teaching especially included how to use Scripture in faithful ways and to avoid a careless use of texts that might serve only to create distance for our friends rather than draw them to the rich story of God's love in Christ.

Pastors must not only teach evangelism but also model what it looks like to live as evangelists. This brings up one of the great challenges for pastors: the danger of becoming so enmeshed in congregational life that they become insulated from the world. Pastors must be exceedingly intentional about building relationships with unchurched people. This is why some pastors in our time are embracing what some have called a *co-vocational* model of ministry. This approach is not so much to meet economic needs as it is to create opportunity for building friendships with people who do not yet confess Christ.

However we go about it, one of the key ways for us as pastors to "do the work of an evangelist" is through modeling in our own lives the utter joy of guiding one of our friends to a life-transforming encounter with the grace of God in Christ. Our mission is to live in such a way that the quality of our lives, individually, in our households, and in the communal life of our congregation announces gospel hope to a world broken by sin. Our work is to call our people to live as ambassadors for Christ, "as though God were making his appeal through us" (2 Cor. 5:20).

13
BEING TEACHER

Jesus was often called Teacher (*rabbi* or *rabbouni* in Aramaic; *didaskalos* in Greek) by his followers. The Gospels present Jesus within the Jewish framework of rabbinic tradition. Yet the Gospels also seem intent on drawing important distinctions between Jesus as teacher and other teachers who often became targets of harsh criticism from Jesus. Matthew 23 includes a list of woes and warnings aimed at teachers who, according to Jesus, lost track of their calling and responsibility. The Lord seems especially perturbed by the eagerness of these teachers to lay burdens on their hearers that they themselves are unwilling to bear with any integrity. This hypocrisy leads Jesus to declare to the teachers of the Law and Pharisees, "You are like whitewashed tombs, which look beautiful on the outside but on the inside are full of the bones of the dead and everything unclean" (v. 27). Clearly, being a faithful teacher is about much more than delivery of content. It has much to do with the character and integrity of the teacher.

Thinking of Jesus as Teacher may first bring to mind the spoken words of our Lord, like the Sermon on the Mount or the parables. Clearly, these words are perhaps the major part of the teaching of Jesus, but the words cannot be separated from the life. Our Lord taught in word *and deed*, and this is paradigmatic for pastors. Jesus certainly taught through discourse. However, these were not lectures focused on the delivery of content but more teaching conversations focused on making disciples. A sign of good teaching is that it creates questions in the minds of the students, prodding them to think more deeply for themselves about the subjects being discussed. This was a common feature of Jesus' teaching as his disciples regularly found themselves wrestling with the things that their teacher was introducing, especially when he taught using parables. It has been suggested that Jesus taught with parables in order to help the people understand his teaching better. If this is true, it did not work very well. Most often, the students of Jesus were left scratching their heads, wondering what in the world he meant with these strange illustrations of life in the kingdom of God. Sometimes, they even became deeply offended and left "the church." Evidently, the teaching strategy of Jesus was about much more than simple delivery of content. Our Lord seemed intent on orchestrating major collisions for people at the intersection of their assumptions or beliefs and the truth of the gospel.

Similarly, pastoral teaching must go deeper than the impartation of facts; it must provide a catalyst for transformative engagement with the gospel. Doing this well requires that pastors understand the teaching role as far more than one component of a complex job description. Pastoral teaching, at its best, is a way of living in the midst of a people whereby one's entire life becomes instructive as a model of fully surrendered discipleship. Before discussing this in detail, however, let us think about being a teacher in the ways we commonly imagine teaching.

Teaching in Worship

The setting of corporate worship certainly provides the pastor with one of the most important venues for teaching. This is true not only in the sermon but also in the whole of the pastor's words and actions as worship leader. Teaching well through worship begins long before the community gathering on Sunday morning. It begins by being mindful in the prayer, reflection, and conversations with others about planning each service of worship that the *entire* experience teaches and shapes our people, like it or not. That is to say, it is not enough to attend to the *explicit* curriculum when planning worship. The explicit curriculum is what we intend to teach; it is the outcome we intend to achieve through all that takes place in the worship service. However, good teachers also attend to the *implicit* curriculum—that which is being taught by implication or even by omission (sometimes called *null* curriculum). For example, if we give far more attention to celebrating Mother's Day than we do to Pentecost Sunday, we are teaching something that I sure hope we did not intend to teach. Or if the elements of the service are presented in a haphazard or careless way, we are teaching that what we are doing here is really not very important. This is not to suggest that we are in charge of every outcome of the worship experience. Jesus is Lord, and the Spirit is in charge of our worship. However, this truth also does not excuse carelessness in planning. If the Spirit can inspire true worship in the moment, the Spirit can also inspire true worship weeks beforehand as pastors pray, study, and plan toward the teachable moments of authentic Christian worship. Therefore, the pastor must give careful attention to every word and action of the worship service.

I have grown immensely weary of services of Christian worship being initiated with the inane greeting, "Good morning!" And to make matters worse, if the people do not sufficiently return the greeting, they are often chided into repeating it louder, "Good morning!" The first words of Christian worship should be a greeting in the name of Jesus Christ the Lord. The first words should be the announcement that we are here today not because we simply decided to come but because we have been gathered by the Spirit. This is teaching. It is reminding our people that our identity is located in our connection to God in Christ and to one another by the presence of the Holy Spirit.

From a proper Christian greeting then, pastors need to think carefully about the movement of every subsequent component of the service. What is the point of this service component? Is this faithful to the Scriptures? Is this faithful to the historic Christian faith? Too often it seems that decisions are made about various components of a service on the basis of little else than what gets a reaction or what will entertain the crowd. What does the intentional presence of Scripture reading teach the congregation, not only through the content but also about the place of the Bible in our worship? It seems ludicrous to hope our people will learn that the Bible is important to their daily lives if it rarely shows up in worship. And when the Bible is read, is it done well? The public reading of Scripture should be done with the intentional preparation of the readers taking place through the week rather than in a brief hallway conversation that morning. Also, if the only persons ever to read Scripture publicly are clergy, we are teaching something that I am not sure we really want to teach. Lay readers of all ages should be prepared and equipped to become excellent and passionate readers of the text in our services of worship. This is all part of the teaching work of a good pastor.

Dare I speak of music? Our persistent temptation with music is to place our focus upon style, instrumentation, and presentation. These are important concerns that can speak to the values of excellence and effective communication. However, if issues of style and spectacle in presentation begin to mute the importance of message and content, we are not exercising care in our teaching. The pastor, the one (or ones) charged with spiritual oversight of the congregation, must never become separated from this work of giving theological oversight to every word that is spoken and sung in the community of faith gathered for worship. Music in worship must be understood to have greater purpose than to evoke feelings. Music teaches, for good or ill. Therefore, great care must be given to what is sung by the people of God. And this is part of the point of teaching. If the people are not engaging the music as participants, the teaching opportunity is probably lost. Too often, I witness congregations being turned into auditors, spectators of a slick presentation happening before them, but not fully engaged participants. Whatever contextual decisions are made concerning style, careful work must be done by pastors to ensure that the singing teaches well. There will be more on worship in the next chapter, but here the point is that every component of the worship service is an important teaching component deserving, perhaps demanding, the attention of the pastor who is theologian in residence.

Teaching in Leadership

Another very important way by which the pastor becomes teacher is through his or her manner of leadership in the life of the congregation. Leadership style is about much more than personality or preference. Every pastor does the work of organizational leadership from a unique set of gifts, strengths, and characteristics of personality. This does not mean, however, that any pastor is doomed to a particular leadership style because of genetics or environment. Pastoral leadership is theological, as I have already argued in chapter 5. Therefore, the particular ways a pastor goes about executing leadership among a congregation is a hugely important component of teaching. Much of what we affirm as true about the nature of Christian community can be harmed by a pastor's careless application of leadership strategies. Unless a pastor is surrendered to the call of the gospel daily, the way he or she leads the church staff or the church board can easily become manipulative, harmful, and antithetical to the clear, biblical descriptions of how relationships should work in the body of Christ (thinking of Rom. 12, for example).

For those pastors who enjoy the assistance of staff members, the relationships of the leadership table should become a microcosm of the quality of relationships we desire to be developed in the whole community of faith. These close relationships can be fraught with peril for many reasons, but it falls on the lead pastor to nurture this small community in ways that enable its life together to become a sign of the kingdom of God for the larger community. This is not only about the skills of interpersonal leadership but significantly about an intentional commitment to good teaching that lives beyond the words. That being said, the words are indeed important. It is especially important in multiple-staff settings that the public and private words of the lead pastor build congregational esteem for and confidence in those who are serving alongside him or her in the pastoral office. It matters when the lead or senior pastor refers to staff colleagues as *pastor.* I spent twelve years assigned as an associate pastor. I had the experience on multiple occasions of visiting parishioners in the hospital or in private residences only to hear, "So nice of you to come, but when is the pastor coming?" Or if they were really trying to encourage me, they would say, "So when are you going to become a real pastor?" I was blessed with leaders who worked to teach the congregation different ways of thinking and talking than this. And when

I had the privilege of working with staff colleagues as a lead pastor, I worked hard to teach our congregation that when any one of us came to the hospital or to private residences to visit, the *pastor* had been there. When any one of us led in various components of the worship service, the *pastor* was leading. This kind of leadership not only builds the esteem of those working with us and builds their vocational confidence but also teaches the congregation something about the nature of leadership in the community of faith. And it teaches the congregation something about the nature of relationships in the church, where we "honor one another above" ourselves (Rom. 12:10).

The pastor's leadership among and relationship with members of the governing board of the congregation is also a tremendous context for teaching. I have been amazed at how many pastors seem to assume that there is an adversarial relationship between pastor and board and that the best they can do is try not to get crossways with board members. This is a defeating way to think about leadership with this group. If this is our mind-set, then an adversarial relationship is what we will likely experience. Regardless of where church polity may place the pastor in relation to church board members, the essential work of a pastor in this setting is to cast biblical vision not only for what the congregation should be doing but also for *how* the congregation should be doing it.

Many local church boards are populated with folks who know how to run things. These are often business leaders, educators, parents, and other leaders who know things about organizational leadership. What they often forget, however, is how to pay attention to where God is working in all of this and how to stay attentive to God in the midst of their decisions about program, finance, and so forth, so that these decisions are faithful to our mission. This requires someone to teach them, and the assignment has been given to the pastor. Consequently, a board discussion about the budget is never just about money. It is always about values, priorities, and the faithful stewardship of all that has been entrusted to the church's care. Decisions about personnel in a congregation can never be judged solely on the basis of performance, productivity, or perceived return on investment. Churches must attend to the fact that how they execute decisions, especially difficult decisions that are painful for some people, speaks a loud and clear message to the community about how they understand themselves and about what they value. These things are so important that they simply cannot be left to chance. They must be shaped, schooled, and taught by a pastor who not only knows the truth but also is willing to speak truth back to the lies of popular culture so easily adopted by our people.

I cannot leave out one more leadership context in which pastors teach: the ways in which pastors relate to those in authority over them. This was discussed in chapter 7, but I think it bears repeating in this context of teaching. Submission to authority seems essential to a healthy, biblical understanding of the Christian life. It is fascinating that pastors who expect their people to respond to their spiritual authority and leadership are often quite reticent to submit to the authority of those over them. Every ordained minister is under authority. Foundationally, pastors are under the authority of Christ, but they are also under the authority of the church. This is not so much about snapping to attention at every utterance of an overseer as it is about expressing respect for the pastoral office. The teaching component of this is found in the fact that congregations seem to know whether or not their pastors live and work under authority and from an attitude of respect for the connection of congregations of which they are a part. The way that a pastor relates to, talks about, and participates in the ecclesial structure that ordained him or her teaches much to a congregation about the core discipleship concern of appropriate submission to authority.

Teaching in Life

One of the most important ways by which a pastor becomes teacher is through example. The discipline of my denomination exhorts, "The minister of Christ is to be in all things a pattern to the flock."[1] It goes on from there to describe the expected qualities of spiritual leadership but also includes practical matters: "in punctuality, discretion, diligence, [and] earnestness."[2] In this regard, pastors must realize that they are teaching through their manner of conduct in all of life and not only when engaging the official duties of the parish. These life patterns can be as momentous as one's relationship with one's spouse (if married) and as mundane as what movie one chooses to see at the multiplex. Contemporary pastors, especially younger pastors, seem to resist this kind of "glass house" examination. Get over it. When you allow the elders of the church to lay hands on you and the bishop to ordain you into the church of God, your life is no longer your own. This is no job choice, no compartmentalized occupation, no nine-to-five life; this is your calling. Once God calls and the church lays hold of you, do not try to escape her grasp. Recognize (and it is possible to recognize with joy) that you not only belong to God but also belong to the church. Therefore, your life teaches one way or the other.

The pastor's familial relationships are a core component of this. For pastors who are married, the relationship of pastor and spouse should not only be a model of Christian marriage but also be a platform from which the people are taught intentionally about the qualities and practices that constitute a healthy marriage relationship. Starla and I made a decision only a few years into our marriage that we would not only be transparent with our people about our life together but also work hard at enjoying a healthy and growing marriage so that we could offer that to the congregation as a gift of love. At the risk of hubris, I would dare say that over the thirty-four years of our marriage and ministry, scores of couples have been helped through the example of our marriage. This is not because we are flawless, of course, but because we have offered the example of God's grace at work in our marriage back to the church as a way of pastoral teaching. Similarly, the pastor's relationships with children, parents, and siblings all can become a powerful teaching tool of some of the most essential qualities of discipleship, such as "love, joy, peace, patience, kindness, goodness, faithfulness, gentleness, [and] self-control" (Gal. 5:22-23, esv). A caution here would be that we must be careful to avoid engaging in these relationships only or primarily with an eye toward what others may see or think. Too many pastors' children have suffered under the burden of "what the church people might think." The only way these familial relationships can teach effectively is when they are authentic and the evidence of this genuineness is carried over time. This is another reason why longer pastoral tenures can be so impactful for a congregation. The congregation we pastored for fourteen years watched us raise children from birth (our youngest) through marriage (our oldest) and navigate before them all of the realities of raising children in a world like ours.

In teaching with one's life, the pastor must also pay attention to how life realities like consumer choices, financial management, and physical health become important lessons of what holiness looks like in the everyday world. With regard to consumer choices, what does my lifestyle communicate to my community about what I value most? Am I simply going along with what popular culture says I should value? Or does my lifestyle communicate a commitment to Christian simplicity? These are not easy decisions to make, and they are indeed quite personal, but for the pastor they are not private.

Regarding financial management, does my lifestyle support my testimony that I do not live for myself but live for the sake of others and work to follow the advice made famous by John Wesley, "Having, First, gained all you can, and, Secondly saved all you can, Then give all you can."[3] Pastors should model generosity. I have encountered far too many pastors who bemoan the financial paucity of their parish, only to discover that the pastors were not giving out of the very resources afforded to them by the parish! My practice as a pastor was not only to participate in the offering during worship but also to share with the people how our family prayed over and made decisions about our giving, especially the sacrificial, "over and above" kind of giving that teaches something about surrender to the lordship of Jesus in material concerns.

Lastly, concerning physical health, what does my physical condition say about the stewardship of my body? Does my lack of physical fitness bear witness to my lack of discipline? There can certainly be other issues at work when a person is obese or unhealthy in other ways, and these need serious medical attention. But if my lack of physical health is due to my own failure to do the things necessary toward being healthy, then I am not teaching well about a discipleship that is balanced and holistic. Just recently, I read through the annual personal goals that were set by the pastors under my oversight for the coming year. A number of them identified physical health goals. I wonder if that has anything to do with the example of an overseer who not only practices physical health disciplines but also regularly talks about the connection between physical health and spiritual health? We are teachers in all of life.

In these ways, and many more, pastors are teachers not only in word but also in deed. Faithful and effective pastoral life will give sufficient attention to this reality and will seek to model Christian discipleship for our people in worship, leadership, and in daily living.

14
BEING OFFICIANT

The pastoral work of officiating, whether in worship and sacraments or in times of key life transitions, is one of the best-loved components of pastoral life. These are also the moments that carry some of the most important influence we can ever have in the lives of the people we are called to serve. It is in fact a beautiful thing to preside over some of the most memorable events in the lives of people we have grown to know and love over years of serving them as pastor. In these cases, the work of pastor as officiant flows from the larger context of life together and, as such, has in view all of the teaching and shaping that is done with a people over time. Many others, however, may only encounter a Christian pastor in connection with a baptism, a wedding, or a funeral. This reality emphasizes the importance of pastors making sure that these occasions are officiated with theological precision and pastoral intention.

Part of the importance of handling these moments well is found in the uncomfortable truth that people are constantly seeking to domesticate pastors. This seems especially true during occasions such as weddings and funerals, which have been largely overtaken by the sentimentalities of popular culture. When it comes to these important life milestones, folks seem all too anxious to turn us into incidental icons. They need us there to make a pronouncement or to offer some kind of spiritual legitimacy to what they are doing, but after that we had better not get in the way of their party. More on these events later, but first we need to think about the pastor as officiant in the most central and essential of all Christian gatherings: worship.

Pastor as Worship Leader

Worship has fallen on hard times in contemporary, evangelical Christianity. Like many other aspects of Christian experience, worship has been seriously co-opted by the entertainment culture. This is evident in our language as the word "worship" is often used simply to describe the part of the service given to music. Entire conferences are held on how to create a "worship experience" that looks and feels like the slick, highly produced entertainments to which people have grown accustomed. But do not misunderstand my concern. All that we do in Christian gathering should be done with the highest quality possible. And I am not bemoaning the loss of one style for another style. My concern here is that in our focus on how the elements of a service are presented, we have too often neglected the essential components that are necessary to call a gathering *Christian worship*. The components are established and may not be casually dismissed in favor of "what people want." The key components of Christian gathering are evident in Scripture and made explicit in the life of the church, including some of the earliest writings of the church fathers. Justin Martyr (AD 150) outlined the movements of worship in his *Apology* (chap. 67) to include these elements:

- Intentional gathering of proximate people on Sunday
- Reading and hearing of Scripture in the assembly
- Exhortation from the presider, based on the readings
- Corporate prayer, especially thanksgiving for the gifts of the Table
- Celebration of the Eucharist
- An offering received for the poor, especially orphans and widows
- Carrying the gifts of the Table to those unable to gather[1]

These movements were rooted in synagogue practices in which our Lord participated (e.g., Luke 4:16). Jesus worked from the life of his worshipping community in instituting the table of the Last Supper, where, in the sharing of blessed bread and wine, disciples are constituted together as the church by the power of the Spirit. While not specifically about Sunday worship, Acts 2:42-47 is often referenced as descriptive of the life of the community of faith, including several of the acts found in Justin's description. The point here is that while the acts of Christian worship may be carried out in creative and engaging ways that are contextualized to communicate to the people to whom we are called, the core components of Christian worship are not subject to revision. It is the responsibility of the pastor to ensure that the gathering of the people of God for worship is truly Christian. So, let us think about pastoral responsibility in these core elements of worship that is authentically Christian.

The first movement in Christian worship is *gathering*, or what some have called *entrance*.[2] Good pastors understand and maximize what this means for their particular congregations. Perhaps the most important idea in thinking about gathering is a theological recognition that a gathering of people only truly becomes the church when they are gathered by the Spirit. This awareness profoundly shapes how we gather, and it should shape the work of pastors long before the physical gathering. Recognizing the prevenient grace of God at work in my community means that as a pastor I will spend much of my time through the week praying into this truth. Pastors pray every day that the Spirit will gather the people of God in worship. This means much more than praying that they will show up. It means joining in the prayer of the church through many centuries, *Veni, Sancte Spiritus*—"Come, Holy Spirit."

Those of us who came into vocational ministry in the era of the "church growth movement" too often think of our work toward Sunday as trying to get a crowd. This could be as substantive as making calls on people, encouraging them to come on Sunday (a good thing to do). Or it could be as silly as promising that if a certain number of people are in church on Sunday, the pastor will suffer some manner of indignity, whether a pie in the face or a scissors to the necktie. The impulse may be understandable; we want people to come and hear the gospel proclaimed.

The problem is that these efforts have a tendency to put the emphasis on our work rather than on the profound truth that the Spirit of the risen Jesus is already working "to seek and to save the lost" (Luke 19:10). This is why it is so important, as mentioned in the previous chapter, that the service of Christian worship begin with something much deeper than, "Good morning!" We hear that greeting in all kinds of gatherings that are not Christian. The entrance to Christian worship should in some way include the words, "Greetings in the name of our risen Lord Jesus Christ." Or perhaps a greeting straight from Scripture: "Grace to you and peace from God our Father and the Lord Jesus Christ" (1 Cor. 1:3).

Many congregations then move immediately to engage the people in the gathering, recognizing our partnership in the gospel through call and response: "The Lord be with you . . . And also with you." However it is done, it must be clear that we have been gathered by God for the purpose of glorifying God. This intentional recognition may become a prophetic word to people who have come with little awareness beyond that of a consumer, judging whether or not they like the show that is about to take place or the services otherwise offered by this religious shop.

Another part of entrance is acts of praise, often through music. As argued earlier, although congregations may have highly skilled people to lead in music, the selection of songs should never be given away entirely by the pastor as the one who is charged to ensure that our singing takes place with theological attention and intention. The opportunity for the pastor to work with musicians in preparation that includes prayerful selection of the music should be viewed as integral to leading worship.

The second major movement in Christian worship is to hear from Scripture. Evangelical tradition, especially as rooted in revivalism, has tended to view this almost exclusively as the sermon. Gladly, there seems to be a resurgence of emphasis upon a broader hearing of Scripture in worship. Various kinds of lectionaries have been used for centuries in the church, and they seem to be finding their way to wider use. The purpose of a lectionary is to help the congregation hear from the whole counsel of God, drawing from Old and New Testaments and including for each Sunday selected texts from History, Psalms, Epistles, and Gospels. These selected texts complement one another and also follow the rhythms of the Christian year. The pastor may or may not select the sermon text from the assigned readings, but following a lectionary helps the life of the community to be grounded in the story of God.[3]

It is vital that the flow of communal life find its moorings not so much in the rhythms of the lunar or civil calendars but in the story of the birth, life, death, resurrection, and ascension of our Lord. The key point is not to get lost in any system but to make sure that the Scriptures are prominent in the acts of the worshipping community. This certainly extends to the sermon, which must be biblical above all else. The service of the Word may also include the collective affirmation of a creedal statement of faith (usually the Apostles' Creed or the Nicene Creed). It also includes significant time for prayer. This can be pastoral prayer where the pastor leads the people to express the praises and petitions of the congregation. It can also be prayers of the people, where petitions are voiced from the congregation and all agree in prayer to plead the mercies and grace of our Lord. However it is done, a key pastoral act is to lead the congregation in prayer, and sufficient time must be given to this, including opportunity (at least on occasion) for the people to be in silence together before the Lord.

Perhaps the most important act of ordained ministry is to offer the sacrament of Communion. Most Christian congregations celebrate the Lord's Supper weekly, understanding the Eucharist as the central act of Christian worship. Other churches, particularly those in the so-called believers church or revivalist tradition, have tended toward less frequent observance. When Communion is understood as more than memorial, but truly as a means of grace, then the impulse is toward more frequent observance. One of the most critical of all pastoral works is to set the Table well. Far too often I have witnessed the offering of the Lord's Supper in haphazard and careless ways. This is among the most sacred of responsibilities that is given to the pastor upon ordination. Therefore, it must be approached with prayerful reverence and disciplined attention to the preparation, blessing, and offering of the elements to the people of God (much more on this in a moment).

There are many other possible components that I have not mentioned here, such as passing of the peace and the offering of gifts.

However, the fourth major component of authentically Christian worship is the sending of the people of God into the world in mission. This can be done in a variety of ways, but some form of intentional benediction or blessing should not be neglected. This was discussed in chapter 12, but the essence of it is the pastor speaking words of blessing over the people as they depart to serve Christ in the world. In recent days I have noticed, as an increasing practice among congregations in my connection, the people lifting their hands, palms turned upward, as the pastor lifts his or her hands toward the people while the words of blessing are spoken. The biblical words of "grace and peace" should be prominent in these acts along with regular teaching about the purpose and meaning of these acts and words.

Worship is in one sense a drama that is played out every week by and among God's people. It is a rehearsal of the grand story of redemption and a renewal of faith in the God who redeems. All of God's people in the gathered community are the actors, and God is the audience. A key role in the weekly drama is enacted in the life of one who was drawn out from this community, ordained and sanctified for priestly ministry, and sent back to the community to pronounce with authority, "Let us worship God." This may be the single most important act, when done with prayerful intention, that a pastor can offer to the world. It is a prophetic call away from the gods of this world and toward the one true God and Father of our Lord Jesus Christ.

The Sacrament of Baptism

As one of two sacraments recognized and practiced by the church, the baptism of new Christians is certainly a central component of the officiating work of pastors. Therefore, it must be done with great care. But how hard can it be to plunge someone beneath the water? You might be surprised, actually. During one of my most memorable baptisms, the candidate who happened to be a man much larger than myself, reached out and grabbed the sides of the baptismal pool as I tried to force his massive body beneath the waters. In the struggle that ensued (while calmly invoking the Trinity) we both got plenty wet. Sometimes the "old man" resists being "buried in baptism."

Seriously, the importance of baptism should be reflected in the preparation that takes place for the candidate. One type of preparation is for the believer who is giving testimony of faith in Christ. Sometimes baptism proceeds immediately upon the profession of faith, but most of the time there is a period of preparation for the baptism. This seems preferable as a way of establishing discipling relationships. In some traditions the baptismal candidate is presented by a mentor or spiritual director who has guided him or her in prayer and study of the Scriptures to prepare for this momentous event. In other cases, the preparation will be with parents who are presenting their child for baptism, committing to nurture their child to choose one day what they are now choosing for him or her. In both cases, one of the most important acts of the pastor is to teach the congregation about the sacrament as an integral part of celebrating the baptism. This is especially true when infants are presented for baptism, since there is much misunderstanding about this in evangelical circles.

Most important is to teach the people that baptism is a sacrament, a means of grace. It is not simply a testimony, although it certainly is a powerful testimony of faith in God. The testimony, however, is to the grace of God in Christ. And the sacrament not only is a celebration of this grace but is, in fact, grace. Something actually happens by faith when a person is plunged beneath the consecrated waters of the baptismal pool and is raised from the waters to be welcomed into the household of faith. This is the sign of entrance into the church. Therefore, baptism should always precede membership in the congregation. Baptism is not an incidental act; it is essential. John Wesley taught it as such. He said, "By baptism we enter into covenant with God . . . By baptism we are admitted into the church, and consequently made members of Christ, its head."[4] A thorough discussion of baptismal theology is beyond the scope of the present work. I recommend the excellent volume by Dr. Rob Staples, *Outward Sign and Inward Grace: The Place of Sacraments in Wesleyan Spirituality* (Beacon Hill Press of Kansas City, 1991).

Strong pastoral teaching and practice on baptism can become a significant part of calling believers into the obedience of baptism. I recall a longtime church member in the congregation I served as pastor whom I discovered had never been baptized. In fact, he resisted it in our early conversations. However, over time he was finally compelled by the experience of witnessing regularly the baptismal teaching of the pastor as part of observing the sacrament, the testimony of those being baptized, and especially the affirmation of the community of faith saying these words to the newly baptized: "We receive you into the household of God. Confess the faith of Christ crucified, proclaim his resurrection, and share with us in his eternal priesthood." In other words, the Spirit who was present and working in the worshipping community faithfully drew him into the waters of baptism.

Practically then, what are some important components of observing the sacrament of baptism? My focus here will be on believer baptism by immersion, being most common in my tradition. First is the recognition that as a sacrament this belongs in the community of faith. Baptism should be celebrated in the church (meaning, the community of Christians). Baptism should take place in the context of the community that will continue to nurture this Christian's life and will be the people to whom this believer offers his or her gifts and accountability. Second, the sacrament of baptism should be a big deal, not an afterthought or tacked on to an otherwise full service. Some churches celebrate baptism at certain times, such as Easter or Pentecost. The value of this is not only time for adequate preparation but also space for a significant service. The service of Christian baptism should include Scripture, teaching, prayer, professions of faith, and significant community participation in the moment. Pastors should give significant attention to the occasion. Having the baptismal candidates dressed in white robes sets them apart in a beautiful way and becomes a part of marking them as members of the church of Jesus Christ. Third, the service should include elements of intentional gathering, perhaps a shared hymn such as "Baptized in Water,"[5] Scripture reading (Rom. 6 is a great choice), and a short homily to teach the meaning and significance of baptism.

Then for the baptism proper, careful pastoral attention to these elements is important in order to administer the sacrament in a faithful way. First, offer a prayer of consecration over the baptismal waters. One example: "Now sanctify this water, we pray you, by the power of your Holy Spirit that those who here are cleansed from sin and born again may continue forever in the risen life of Jesus Christ our Savior. To him, to you, and to the Holy Spirit, be all honor and glory, now and forever."[6] Next, the candidates together should be addressed and examined. One such examination is expressed in this way:

> Pastor: "Do you now renounce everything that would draw you away from the love of God?"
>
> Candidates: "I do."
>
> Pastor: "Do you now turn to Jesus Christ and accept him as your Savior? Do you put your whole trust in his grace and love? Do you promise to follow and obey him as your Lord?"
>
> Candidates: "I do. Jesus Christ is Lord."

As each candidate then comes into the baptismal pool, he or she is invited to profess faith in Jesus Christ, to give testimony of God's grace that has drawn him or her into the life of Christ by faith. Then the baptism might include these words and acts:

> Pastor: "(Name), upon your profession of faith in Christ, you are baptized in the name of the Father, the Son, and of the Holy Spirit."

Following the immersion, another practice from Christian history is anointing with oil. The pastor may make the sign of the cross on the candidate's forehead with oil and say, "Receive the healing and grace of our Lord Jesus Christ." Then, the pastor laying hands on the head of the newly baptized could pronounce this blessing: "And may the power of the Holy Spirit be with you, that having been born of water and the Spirit, you may be a faithful follower of our Lord Jesus Christ." At this point, it is important for the congregation to affirm and welcome the newly baptized with words echoing those mentioned above and spoken together in unison: "We receive you into the household of God. Confess the faith of Christ crucified, proclaim his resurrection, and share with us in his eternal priesthood."

Obviously, the baptism of infants would contain unique acts, such as sprinkling or pouring the water. There may also be a charge given to the parents and to the community of faith eliciting their commitment to raise this child in a way that nurtures the child toward a profession of faith in Jesus Christ as Savior. A related issue that needs careful attention among pastors is the inevitable request of someone who was baptized earlier in life to be rebaptized upon a fresh embrace and expression of faith. The emotions surrounding this are often strong, and these conversations must be handled with great pastoral care and wisdom. However, the pastor must help the church understand that baptism is a once-for-all sacrament as the way of entrance into the church. Communion, by contrast, is a regular sacrament as a means of nurture in the faith. To rebaptize is to put the emphasis on us (testimony) rather than on God (prevenient grace). And baptism belongs to the church of Jesus Christ, not to any particular denomination. Therefore, when one has been baptized into Christ, one has been baptized into Christ, period! Rebaptism is biblically, theologically, and historically contrary not only to a Wesleyan understanding of the sacrament but to the whole of Christian thought and practice.

Therefore, when someone declares a desire for rebaptism, the pastoral task is to guide the person toward a meaningful and significant reaffirmation of his or her baptism. This should also be done in the community of faith and as a part of the celebration of the sacrament of baptism. Part of that service can be to celebrate the reaffirmation of baptism for those who perhaps fell away from Christ and the church for a time and have been reclaimed. Reaffirmation celebrates the prevenient grace of God that always scans the horizon, looking for the return of the lost one. The liturgy can be very similar to that for those being baptized by including the examination and professions of faith and testimony. Rather than being baptized again, however, the candidate for reaffirmation could receive a pronouncement such as, "(Name), the Lord defend you with his heavenly grace and by his Spirit confirm you in the faith and fellowship of all true disciples of Jesus Christ. Amen." The acts of anointing and blessing could also be offered as part of the reaffirmation liturgy. Celebrating these kinds of acts in the community strengthens our theology of the sacrament and continues to teach our people that the essence of baptism is not our testimony but the grace of God in Christ.

The Sacrament of Communion

As discussed above, offering the Eucharist may be the most important act of ordained ministry. Therefore, it demands careful pastoral attention so that this gift of God is offered to the church in a manner that is faithful to the Scriptures and to the life of the church. The pastor needs to set the Table well, and certain elements are crucial. Certainly, there are varieties of liturgies. My denomination offers particular ritual language that most of our pastors follow. This is wise and keeps us from becoming inappropriately inventive with the handling of the sacrament.

Part of setting the Table well has to do with the context in which the sacrament is celebrated. Here, as in baptism, it is important to be attentive to the fact that this sacrament is a gift to the church and therefore must be celebrated in the context of the worshipping community. It is also important that the offering of Communion be presided over by an ordained minister. Others may be involved in the distribution or serving of elements, but the celebrant proper should be ordained or properly recognized by one's ecclesial authority as a minister of the gospel.

Preparation of the elements may be done by lay ministers but should be supervised by the pastor in the sense that this sacred responsibility is not approached with carelessness. Some instruction should be given for those who prepare the elements, including the instruction to do so prayerfully. The manner of serving the elements may be varied, and congregations may use several methods of serving. Theologically, it may be most preferred to invite worshippers forward to receive the elements from the minister(s). Some do this by intinction, the worshipper dipping the bread into the cup and partaking. The strength of this method is the use of a common loaf and common cup that speaks of our unity in Christ at the Table. At other times it may be necessary to distribute the elements, usually by wafers and cups for each worshipper. One way to keep track of our unity in this method is by asking the congregation after receiving the elements to wait until all have been served and then worshippers receive the bread and cup together.

Of great importance in offering the sacrament of Communion is the invitation to the Table. The words of invitation from the discipline of my church are:

The Lord himself ordained this holy sacrament. He commanded His disciples to partake of the bread and wine, emblems of His broken body and shed blood. This is His table. The feast is for His disciples. Let all those who have with true repentance forsaken their sins, and have believed in Christ unto salvation, draw near and take these emblems, and, by faith, partake of the life of Jesus Christ, to your soul's comfort and joy. Let us remember that it is the memorial of the death and passion of our Lord; also a token of His coming again. Let us not forget that we are one, at one table with the Lord.[7]

Following the invitation there should be a time for prayerful reflection and confession, perhaps including a corporate prayer of preparation. One such prayer that I found helpful as a pastor was to guide our people in the Collect for Purity:

Almighty God, to whom all hearts are open, all desires known, and from whom no secrets are hidden: Cleanse the thoughts of our hearts by the inspiration of your Holy Spirit that we may perfectly love you, and worthily magnify your holy name; through Jesus Christ our Lord. Amen.[8]

Many congregations also join together in a responsive reading of "The Great Thanksgiving" from the Book of Common Prayer, which can be a significant way to prepare the hearts of the congregation to receive Communion in a proper frame. This usually leads directly to the words of institution, whereby the pastor reminds the people from Scripture (usually 1 Cor. 11) of how our Lord instituted this holy sacrament with his disciples. At this point one of the most important acts of the pastor comes into view. Perhaps the greatest responsibility and privilege for the ordained minister in the celebration of this sacrament is to give the words of *epiclesis* (calling down from above), a prayer for the coming of the Holy Spirit:

> Pour out your Holy Spirit on us gathered here, and on these gifts of bread and wine. Make them be for us the body and blood of Christ that we may be for the world the body of Christ, redeemed by his blood. By your Spirit make us one with Christ, one with each other.[9]

Now the officiant breaks the bread as a sign of the body of Christ broken for the sake of the world. This act may include words such as, "We break this bread to share in the body of Christ." Some pastors do this in connection with the words of institution, saying,

> We are reminded that in the same night that our Lord was betrayed, He took bread and, when He had given thanks, He broke it [celebrant tears the bread] and gave it to His disciples, saying, "This is my body given for you; do this in remembrance of me." Likewise, after supper, He took the cup [celebrant lifts the cup], and when He had given thanks, He gave it to them, saying, "This cup is the new covenant in my blood, which is poured out for you; do this, whenever you drink it, in remembrance of me."[10]

Now the elements and the congregation are properly prepared for the distribution. Servers should be instructed to say to those coming to receive these elements, "The body of Christ broken for you" and "the blood of Christ shed for you." Usually the worshipper responds with, "Thanks be to God." Please do not miss the point in all of this. The issue is not about following a script to the letter. It is about approaching this most sacred of acts in the life of the church with care and prayerful intention. It is about remembering that we did not think of this last week. This is a gift of the historic Christian faith that has been carefully handed down to us century by century, millennium by millennium. We simply are not authorized to innovate to the point that this connection is lost. Keeping track of this is the responsibility of the pastor as officiant.

Weddings and Funerals

Although not recognized as sacraments in much of the church, these two moments are extremely significant times in the life of the community of faith when the pastor must attend to what it means to be officiant. They are also fraught with peril in contemporary contexts, having been so thoroughly hijacked by consumer-driven sentimentality and an increasingly common pagan worldview. Consequently, these events are not only significant ritual moments that pastors must handle carefully but also important teachable moments, pregnant with opportunity to correct folk theology and market-driven values.

The Christian Wedding

The wedding may be the most dangerous event of all for a pastor. The legend of *Bridezilla*[11] has now been well documented by cable television. And far scarier than Bridezilla herself is Bridezilla's mother! One of my favorite print cartoons shows two women sitting in a pew together at a wedding, the pastor and couple standing before them. One woman, whom we discern is the pastor's wife, leans over to her seatmate and says, "He really prefers funerals. He is far more certain they are in God's will." In the United States, weddings have become, by some estimates, a $40 billion industry annually, with the average wedding cost at somewhere around $26,000.[12] In light of the energy and expense most families are investing in this spectacle, is it any wonder that the preacher is viewed as fairly marginal? As the old joke goes, being the preacher at a wedding is like being the corpse at a funeral visitation. They can't have the party without you, but no one really expects you to say very much.

A wedding is one of the most important moments in which pastors must resist being domesticated. Not long ago I sat with a young couple to talk about their wedding, which they had invited me to officiate. Like every couple I have ever encountered at that point, they were full of idealized sentimentality and gushing with excitement over their big day. So I began our meeting with, "I really do not care about your wedding." Their smiles drooped into frowns. "What I care about," I continued, "is your marriage, and that is what I want to talk to you about." There is much that should be said right here about the premarital process, including counseling. It will have to suffice here to say that part of pastoral responsibility is to prepare the couple as much as possible so that when the prophetic words of the wedding liturgy are spoken, they will resonate as familiar not only to those who are making vows on that day but also to all who have ever made the vows of marriage and have come to witness these new vows. This begs the observation that like the sacraments proper, the "sacrament" of marriage belongs to the church and should be celebrated in the context of the community of faith. There is no such thing as a private wedding. And as a pastor, I strongly resisted weddings taking place in settings other than the regular gathering place of that community of faith. When weddings are relocated to venues that are chosen simply because they serve the interests of the "party" rather than the interests of the church, something is misplaced. The point is not to become legalistic about location but to keep this sacred moment vitally connected to the church. The truth is, pastors will not always (perhaps rarely) be able to change the mind of the bride (and bride's mother) on this point, but it should not go without saying and is part of being a prophetic voice in the midst of this significant moment.

Prior to thinking about the ceremony proper, another important thing to say to pastors presiding at weddings is this: you are *not* a part of the bridal party. You are not there to fit in, facilitate every whim, or hurry it up so they can get on with the party. You are there as vicar (representative) of Christ.

I once had a bride beg me to dress in a certain way, wearing certain colors so that I would "fit it" with the bridal party and the overall décor of the event. I am quite sure she was offended when I refused. And I know her mother was incensed! For this reason, although not common in my tradition, I began to wear a clerical robe for the wedding ceremony. This is a way to declare visually that the pastor belongs to something other than this event—that he or she indeed represents the church under whose authority this event is taking place. Above all, be very clear about this: the authority to solemnize marriage comes only from Christ and the church. It does not come from the state of anywhere. The state may recognize our authority to solemnize marriage and allow us to sign the legal document to verify the union. However, while the state takes authority to *legalize* marriage, only the church has authority to *solemnize* marriage. Therefore, when a bride and groom stand before a Christian pastor for the solemnization of marriage, they are coming under the authority of the church of Jesus Christ. The bride has been told time and time again that this day is all about her, but she was told wrong. The preparation events, gifts, clothing, flowers, and reception may all be about her (poor groom), but once we move into the sanctuary, the pastor is absolutely in charge. This has to be established long before the wedding day and should be a part of careful preparation, including strong guidance in the choosing of Scripture texts, songs, and other elements of the ceremony.

In the ceremony, there are several important matters to which the careful pastor will attend. Chief among these is that the ceremony is framed clearly as a gathering of Christian worship. If this cannot be done, then the pastor has no business being part of it. Undoubtedly, there will be unbaptized persons in attendance, but this is also true (hopefully) in the worship gatherings of the church. When a Christian pastor is presiding, the service should be declared from the beginning as belonging to God and taking place under the gaze of Christ by the presence of the Holy Spirit. ·

I was recently told of a couple desiring to be married that decided, under the godly counsel of their pastor, to have their wedding during the Sunday worship service of their community of faith. The sensational and sentimental trappings of contemporary weddings were all avoided in favor of the church family at worship celebrating the covenant of Christian marriage with their sister and brother in the Lord. If this kind of rootedness to the life of the church were to become the norm, I wonder how it might impact the health of all marriages.

Having then established this gathering as Christian worship, the gospel should be proclaimed. This does not have to be and should not be a long or complicated sermon. It should, however, be a clear and concise biblical message about the kind of self-sacrificing love that is the gospel and on which the covenant of marriage is based. It is my conviction that the pastor should not give away too many components of the ceremony. It may be fine to have a family member who also happens to be clergy to participate in some way. However, the pastor who is officiating must give clear leadership to what is happening, including the reading of Scripture and prayers. It is not uncommon for Christian couples to desire the celebration of the Eucharist during a wedding ceremony. On one hand, this is understandable and perhaps appropriate when the celebration is deeply linked to the couple's community of faith. On the other hand, unless this service is clearly established as Christian worship, the sacrament of Communion can easily be abused. The most common of these abuses is when the consecrated elements are offered only to the couple while all others simply watch. This should never be done. Holy Communion is a gift to the church and as such should always be celebrated in the gathered community of faith with the invitation to all of Christ's disciples to receive the gifts of bread and wine. When the couple decides to celebrate Eucharist in this way as part of their wedding, the pastor must be careful to set the Table in the ways described above, particularly with words of institution and proper consecration of the elements.

Other pastoral concerns during the wedding involve the pronouncement. Given the observation above that the solemnizing of marriage is under the authority of the church, a pastor should never say what I have sometimes heard pastors say at the climactic moment: "By the authority vested in me by the state of _____ . . ." The authority should be explicitly and clearly stated, "As a minister of the gospel in the church of Jesus Christ, I do now pronounce you husband and wife; in the name of the Father, the Son, and the Holy Spirit." Following this pinnacle moment, the eager groom is often invited to greet his bride with a kiss. But do not forget, either before the kiss or before the presentation, to pronounce benediction over this newly formed living sign of God's covenant love. Although these occasions are indeed perilous, they truly are potentially joyful moments in which pastoral relationships are deepened for a lifetime.

The Christian Funeral

Unfortunately, funerals have also been fairly overtaken by popular notions of death, grief, and life after death. Even funerals that are strongly located in the church under the guidance of Christian pastors have too often devolved into sentimental memorial services, entirely focused on the deceased or upon the grieving family and friends, with barely a nod to the gospel of resurrection. One of the most important books of late in practical theology is from Thomas Long, *Accompany Them with Singing*. This is a must-read for pastors. Dr. Long writes, "Pastors have tried to make funerals more pastorally sensitive, more comforting to the grief-stricken, but have allowed them to become controlled by psychological rather than theological categories and, therefore, shallower in meaning."[13] I will not try to replicate or even summarize Long's stellar work, but there are a few key notes that the pastor seeking to be a faithful officiant should remember.

While the funeral service should focus on proclamation of the gospel, the period leading up to and just after the passing of a loved one are certainly some of the most important and meaningful of pastoral encounters. This is a time when a pastor just cannot miss the opportunity to be present in substantive ways. This does not necessarily mean hovering over the situation constantly, but it does mean being in regular contact and helping the loved ones to know that they are not alone. Of course, the larger faith community should be involved in this, and some laypeople have special gifts in these moments. However, nothing can replace the prayerful presence of the pastor when life and death meet so clearly. The primary function of the pastor in these moments is to pray. The temptation is to get engaged in conversations about medical details or other details of the death and all that follows. Certainly, pastoral advices can be helpful in these moments, but the pastor must never lose sight of the primary ministry he or she has to offer in these moments. The pastor is there to represent Christ, to name God in the midst of this grief, and to pray the ministry of the Comforter into the situation.

Ministry to the family following the death of a loved one can and should include the gathering of memories and the telling of stories.

Some of these may even find their way into the funeral service. The challenge is to make sure that the primary focus of the funeral service is on the message of Christian hope, on the good news of resurrection. Having attended numerous funeral services, I have instructed members of my own family ("pleaded with" may be more accurate) to keep the memoirs mostly to the visitation time prior to the funeral service and the fellowship dinner after the service. In those events, they may go ahead and tell all the stories and show all the photos. But on entering the sanctuary, they must understand that it is a service of Christian worship where the gospel of resurrection is clearly proclaimed. People have been profoundly shaped by popular notions of what constitutes an appropriate funeral. Consequently, the pastor usually has serious work to do to cast a different and more Christian vision for what should constitute a Christian funeral.[14]

The best funeral I attended recently was for a retired professor of Nazarene Theological Seminary in Kansas City. The service began with the voice of one of his colleagues declaring as he led the casket down the chapel aisle, "I am the resurrection and the life" (John 11:25). The bell was sounded loud and clear that this was to be no ordinary memorial service. This was a gospel service wherein the people of God would remember our sure foundation who is Jesus Christ, the crucified, resurrected, and ascended Son of God "who is at the right hand of God, who indeed is interceding for us" (Rom. 8:34, ESV). The service proceeded with songs of hope and faith, Scriptures bearing witness to our redemption, and prayers of thanksgiving for the hope that is ours in Christ. Then in perhaps the finest funeral sermon I have heard, the preacher proclaimed the truth of our hope, "For as in Adam all die, so in Christ all will be made alive" (1 Cor. 15:22). As an authentically Christian funeral, it delivered more comfort and peace than any sentimental memorial I have ever witnessed. As pastors we are charged to lead our congregations to Christ. One of the strongest opportunities we have is in the death of saints who bear witness to us that we are preparing to join that great company of saints who are with the Lord, awaiting the resurrection.

Difficult funerals for a pastor are when the deceased is one who made no known profession of faith in Jesus Christ. Here the opportunity remains and perhaps intensifies to preach the gospel. The worst thing a pastor can do in this moment is to seek the comfort of loved ones through painting a false portrait of the deceased. I saw a car bumper sticker once that read, "Live so that the preacher doesn't have to lie at your funeral." Well, preacher, do not lie but tell the truth that is the glorious hope of our faith. These moments provide the community of faith with a wonderful and regular opportunity to "give an answer to everyone who asks you to give the reason for the hope that you have" (1 Pet. 3:15).

15
BEING RECONCILER

"Where two or three gather in my name" (Matt. 18:20) a fight will soon break out. Conflict is inevitable in any relationship where people are actually on a journey of knowing each other. For this reason, conflict is not necessarily a bad thing. On the quest toward intimacy, two or more people will sooner or later discover that they have a difference about something. Add strong feelings to this difference, and we have conflict. The presence of conflict does not really mean that something is wrong; it means that we are facing an opportunity for growth in our relationship as we navigate our difference.

My wife and I have done a lot of work in marriage enrichment ministry over the years. We have worked with perhaps hundreds of couples on skills for improving their marriages and enjoying greater intimacy through effective communication. We have worked with couples on the brink of divorce and couples that enjoy the healthiest of relationships. Regardless of maturity and health, some conflict is part of every marriage. We worry most when a couple says, "Oh, we never fight." This means one of two things. Either they are simply lying or, more likely, they have pulled off to the side of the road on the journey of intimacy. They decided, probably slowly over time, that navigating inevitable conflict in healthy ways was not worth the effort, so they stopped growing. Now their marriage is like a minefield. They have marked the areas and issues that are too volatile to touch, and now they carefully tiptoe around the very differences that hold the greatest potential for their growth. Even while living in the minefield, a couple can come to believe that they have no conflict because they have become experts at avoiding the mines. The problem comes when someone inadvertently steps on one of those mines, and a terrible explosion happens that can cause great harm. The better way of conflict management is for a couple to face the differences, deal honestly with the powerful emotions that usually accompany conflict, and then learn how to negotiate the differences so that both spouses are not only able to live in peace but actually grow as persons and together in their relationship.

Conflict is as old as the church. The disciples of Jesus had plenty. Even the great apostle Paul knew some things about conflict. He experienced sharp disagreements with Barnabas, Peter, and others. We also see at least some evidence that they learned how to navigate and resolve these conflicts in a healthy way (Acts 15, for example). Congregations are like marriages when it comes to conflict. While conflict is inevitable and part of the life of every congregation, Christian communities are not necessarily skilled at working through conflict in productive ways so that they can grow and become more mature. Healthy conflict resolution is a learned skill. Some congregations may have learned to pretend that they do not have conflict. Others are embroiled in unresolved conflict to the point that it damages their witness and harms the vitality of their fellowship.

This is another place where the work of a good and godly pastor is crucial. Every pastor who arrives in an established congregation inherits a story that includes how the people have dealt with conflict. The way that any congregation deals with conflict is largely a function of how pastoral leaders have understood and executed their role at peacemakers and reconcilers. Most pastors know what it is to find themselves unexpectedly and sometimes unwillingly right in the middle of conflict between parishioners. There are times when pastors may be tempted to don the striped garb of referees in athletic competitions. But rather than simply playing the role of referee and helping people find at least some sort of tenuous peace, what would it mean for the pastor to be reconciler? Clearly, our triune God is reconciler. God the Father sends the Son to reconcile the world to himself, making possible the new creation (2 Cor. 5). We also learn in this text that the ministry of reconciliation is ongoing and that we who have been united to Christ by faith now share in the ministry of reconciliation, "as though God were making his appeal through us" (v. 20).

Surely, we understand this reconciliation to be holistic. It is not only about reconciling us with regard to sin and forgiveness but also about bestowing on us the grace-enabled capacity to become ambassadors of reconciliation. We who are in Christ, who by faith and work of the Spirit constitute the body of Christ, are empowered to be a living sign whereby the quality of our life together announces the in-breaking kingdom of God, a kingdom of reconciliation and peace. And when we as God's people live together in these ways, we become an answer to the prayer of our Lord, who prayed that we might be unified in the same way the Father, Son, and Spirit are unified for the redemption of the world (John 17).

Strategies toward Reconciliation

Our people do not naturally attend to these truths in their relationships with one another. Someone must exhort them, and someone must teach them. Someone must hold them to account for these things, and someone must model a life of reconciliation and peace before them. This someone, of course, is their pastor. Certainly, the pastor is not the only one to do these things, but the pastor must lead the way and must offer intentionality to the community of faith for living into this vision of unity. Accordingly, there are several ways good pastors can do the work of reconciliation in and through their congregations.

First and perhaps most essential is that pastors can model reconciliation in their own lives. The nature of congregational leadership can present many threats to reconciliation and peace. As pastors work to give leadership and to cast vision for the community of faith, it is inevitable that some people will not agree with the vision being cast or the direction being given. Occasionally, folks even begin to feel strongly about their disagreements. Conflict! So what do pastors do when faced with conflicts that in one sense are created by their attempts to lead their congregations faithfully? There are some specific strategies for navigating conflict Christianly, but before talking about those, there is one key component that needs careful attention. It is the willingness of pastors to lay down their lives in service to others.

I often have opportunity to counsel with pastors who find themselves in the midst of conflict with parishioners or perhaps an entire congregation. We discuss many ideas and strategies for resolving the conflicts, but often I say to the pastors under my care, "Remember, you do not have to win." I say this because it is not uncommon, especially for those with a God-given competitive spirit, to come at these conflicts with a passionate desire to come out on top. We want to win partly because we are so completely convinced that we are right. And we may in fact be right. Usually we even have Scripture on our side. But there is something more at stake than being right. There are certainly times when we must insist on being right, as when defending the core doctrines of the church. There are many other times, however, when the strongest position of pastoral leadership is to lay down our will or our rights in surrender to brothers or sisters in Christ. Pastors are usually gifted with strong abilities in organizational leadership. However, we are not called to win; we are called to lay down our lives in sacrificial service to one another. If pastors are allowing unresolved conflict to poison relationships in their own lives—whether familial, congregational, or with neighbors—there is no way they can lead their congregations to the grace of reconciliation and peace.

It should be noted here that congregational dysfunction is not always a sign of the pastor's lack of leadership. There are times when systemic congregational conflict is the result of generational sin and disobedience. Whatever its cause, the task for pastors is to lead people through the steps of navigating conflict Christianly so that they might arrive at authentic reconciliation. These steps begin with a commitment to the rule of Jesus, "So in everything, do to others what you would have them do to you, for this sums up the Law and the Prophets" (Matt. 7:12). This commitment must be embraced by individuals and by congregations. The second step is prayer in which we invite the Holy Spirit to search our hearts and to help us surrender our own interests to the interests of others. The third step may be to confront directly with love. Matthew 18:15-17 gives us helpful direction at this point, especially when facing something that is so common in congregational conflict. People have a tendency to talk to everyone except the person with whom they are having the disagreement. I become aware of this in my work regularly when laypeople call me to complain about their pastor. I have learned that my very first response needs to be, "Now when you spoke to your pastor directly about your concern, what was the response?" You could predict that most often this first conversation has not happened. Good pastoral work can emerge by facilitating these direct conversations between people who simply do not have, for many reasons, the capacity to do it themselves. This is not easy work and can be quite dangerous, but it can also be exceedingly fruitful as the pastor models how a Christian works through conflict.

A fourth and critical step in guiding people through conflict is in the matter of forgiveness. It is not unusual that our differences and how we handle them can create a level of hurt and pain that simply cannot be smoothed over without intentional acts and words of giving and receiving forgiveness. Pastors must remind our people of the hard words of Jesus when he said, "If you forgive anyone's sins, their sins are forgiven; if you do not forgive them, they are not forgiven" (John 20:23). I have often asked people who struggle to forgive, believing their offense and anger to be justified, "Are you willing to receive from God only the level of forgiveness that you are willing to offer to others?" Forgiveness opens a necessary step in the process of conflict resolution. Before we can ever get to the place of negotiating the difference, the negative emotions that so often attend conflict must be dealt with. Sometimes this can happen through clear communication that focuses on sharing one's own experience rather than seeking to lay blame on another. Often dealing with negative emotions in conflict may necessarily include intentional acts of forgiveness, and this is a place where the loving and patient work of a godly pastor can bear much fruit. It is hard work, but the power of forgiveness is profound and central to how people can live together in reconciliation.

When these important steps have been attended to, then we are ready actually to negotiate the difference that created the conflict. One way of thinking about this is that there are really only three possibilities for resolving a conflict. The first is through *conciliation*. This is where one of the parties agrees to come over to the other person's viewpoint. In order for this to be authentic reconciliation, the conciliation must be from love and grace-enabled sacrifice rather than from coercion.

A second way of resolving conflict is through *compromise*. Generally, folks are familiar with the idea of compromise, but it is important to recognize that effective compromise need not be meeting in the exact middle. It could be that someone gives a lot and the other gives only a little. However, when done in love for the sake of reconciliation and peace, this can be an effective and authentic manner of resolution.

A third way of resolution may not seem like resolution at all; it is *coexistence*. This happens when after serious and sustained effort to find resolution through one of the first two options, the parties come to realize that at least for this time they are approaching this issue so differently, the best they can do right now is to agree to disagree. This is a temporary solution, but it can be authentic resolution in the sense that the parties agree that their difference will no longer pull them apart. They will offer grace to each other so that their difference, though passionately experienced, will not become the foothold of divisive speech or actions between them.

My reason for summarizing these exceedingly practical strategies is that when we think of pastors as reconcilers, the temptation would be to overspiritualize the work. This could take several forms, but among them might be either shaming people into submission so that there is an appearance of peace or by telling people that if only they were truly spiritually mature, they would not be in conflict with one another. Neither of these strategies is true or helpful. Therefore, while the work of reconciliation certainly does begin in prayer and careful teaching from the Scriptures, it also must attend to the realities of interpersonal communication and organizational dynamics.

This is not to do something other than pastoral work. It is using the tools of the psychosocial helping arts to accomplish, under the power of the Spirit, the purposes of the kingdom of God.

Perhaps most importantly, to speak of pastors as reconcilers is to recognize that pastors are simply agents of the Holy Spirit in the work of God's reconciliation offered to the world through the life, death, and resurrection of Jesus Christ. Recognizing this, however, in no way minimizes pastors' work of reconciliation, for we are indeed by virtue of our calling and ordination representatives of Christ in the church and in the world. Consequently, we need to pray much in order to resist this world's way of handling conflict. The ability to lay down our lives, surrendering our own need to be right or to win over to the greater good of serving one another in love, requires much prayer. May the Lord help us as pastors to be peacemakers and ambassadors of reconciliation.

16
BEING TRUE

Integrity is named as a high value in many areas of life. The language of integrity has become common in business literature and in the disciplines of organizational leadership. The idea of ethical leadership as a learning discipline is gaining acceptance and use across a fairly wide variety of professional and social contexts. Part of this contemporary interest is no doubt spurred by several very public and egregious failures in leadership, some of which were profoundly costly to global economic stability. While the demand for integrity and ethical behavior among business and governmental leaders may have sharpened in focus over the past decade, people have always expected that ministers of the gospel would operate with the highest levels of integrity and ethics.

Unfortunately, too often this has not been the case. In 1987 two highly public failures of prominent preachers (Jimmy Swaggart and Jim Bakker) helped deepen a growing skepticism in the United States about organized religion in general and the character of spiritual leaders in particular. An already eroding public confidence in the clergy took a nosedive. According to a 2012 Gallup poll, clergy ranked eighth in public assessment of "honest and ethical standards," behind nurses, engineers, and police officers.[1] Since 1977, the high mark in Gallup's poll was in 1985 when 67 percent of respondents assessed clergy with a "very high or high" rating for honesty and ethical standards. The low point was 2009, when 52 percent of respondents gave clergy those higher ratings. I note these data simply to point out that an assumption of integrity is a poor basis from which to inspire the confidence of people that we are who we say we are and actually believe what we say we believe and preach. Our calling is to be so true that the quality of our lives becomes a significant component of proclaiming the gospel of transformed lives by the grace of God in Christ.

Integrity is generally understood as having to do with honesty in that there is authentic agreement between my words and my deeds. I practice what I preach. I suspect that nearly every pastor would affirm the importance of this, and most of us would probably assert that we are people of high integrity. But this does not happen by default. It is intentional. So how can pastors develop in integrity so that the risk of decisions or behaviors that would lead to what is often called *moral failure* among pastors is reduced? What are the key ethical traps for clergy? One could certainly speak of behavioral pitfalls in pastoral ministry that should be avoided. Among these may be the avoidance of impropriety in dealing with finances or in relationships with people of the opposite gender. However, I think there is a deeper concern for first consideration, which is based on a commitment to character or virtue-centered ethics rather than simply principle-centered or *duty* ethics.

Ethical Traps for Clergy

This is where the problem of identity bifurcation comes into view, and this is potentially a serious problem, even for good and godly pastors. The problem arises from the temptation discussed in chapter 5 of our people to idolize pastors and also from the temptation of pastors to accept the idolatrous attitudes and behavior of our people. Regardless of how close we may be to some parishioners, no one outside of a spouse likely has any real idea of whether or not there is authentic correspondence between our public self and our private self. Part of the danger is located in the possibility that pastors may begin to believe the caricature that congregations inevitably develop of their pastors. Perhaps a worse danger is when pastors lose awareness that this is happening. We begin to "believe our own press," as they say in the public relations business. The best way to avoid this bifurcation of identity is by taking the initiative to tell the truth about ourselves.

This can take a number of forms, from self-deprecating humor to serious confession of our sin. Clearly, pastors must exercise wisdom and discernment about how and when to do this. Careless confession before an entire congregation could surely do more harm than good, and this is why serious and authentic accountability is such an important component in pastoral integrity (more on this in a moment).

Another serious ethical trap rises when pastors begin to do their work as technology. What I mean by *technology* in this regard is reliance upon pragmatism. It is going about ministry with a "whatever works" value system taking precedence over what is right according to biblical pastoral theology. This often happens when pastors succumb to the temptation to be seen as successful by the organization. There is no doubt that even today the pastors who tend to be most honored and elevated by denominational hierarchy and by popular church culture are the pastors who lead congregations to experience remarkable growth in attendance and membership. (This may include those who become remarkable by their contrarian or eccentric bearing.) Leading a congregation in significant numerical growth may in fact be worthy of honor, but it may also be worthy of rebuke. *How* things are done matters, and the end does not necessarily justify the means, especially in Christian mission. Our motives must constantly be up for review by God and by those closest to us so that we do not fall to the powerful temptation of "success" for its own sake. True pastoral integrity has much to do with a commitment to have no compromise with worldly systems of power and success.

Another potential ethical trap for clergy is what I will call the consuming of gifts. This can happen in a number of ways. One way is when pastors begin to approach financial resources, especially compensation, with a sense of entitlement. While congregations do have a biblical and moral obligation to care for their pastors in the basic needs of life, pastors must exercise great caution here that they would not ever come under the condemnation of being a "lover of money" (1 Tim. 3:3). The highest level of integrity in this regard may come in a pastor's constant awareness that every dollar he or she receives from pastoral work is a dollar someone placed in an offering with the confidence that it would be used in support of the ministry. Although pastors certainly can do the normal things of life such as caring for their families and even enjoying appropriate diversions, they must also be above reproach regarding either lavish or careless lifestyles. The idea of *lavish* would need to be defined by one's ministry context, and *careless* is about living above one's means and failing to exercise the basic disciplines of resource management.

Interpersonal relationships are another key area in which pastors can sometimes succumb to the temptations to consume rather than steward carefully the gifts of family and friends. For example, pastors must be exceedingly careful that they do not use their family to enhance their own position or standing in the community. This is too often done by pastors placing inappropriate expectations and pressures on their spouses or children to do certain things, behave in certain ways, or perform according to pastoral expectations rather than from each family member's own obedient response to God. Many testimonies exist of the children or spouses of pastors who crumbled under the weight of the pastor's constant reminders to "look the part" in any number of ways. My own pastoral practice has been to remind the congregation that I have but one expectation for my family and it is the same expectation that I have for each person in the church: to live in obedience to whom God is asking them to be and what God is asking them to do.

This area of relationships is also where sexual ethics comes in. Unfortunately, the moral failures that lead to clergy being placed under discipline and sidelined from active ministry are very often failures of sexual integrity. Having worked with colleagues in several of these situations, I have come to understand these failures not so much as prurient sexual interests but more as attitudes of entitlement and self-interested consumption of the good gifts of God. Part of what I have in mind here is my own observation that whenever the moral failure of a pastor includes sexual sin, the use of pornography is discovered regularly to be a starting point. I understand that this is a complex issue, but the point I am drawing here is that under the relentless pressures and demands of pastoral ministry, combined with its attendant stresses on marriage, pastors are vulnerable to a mind-set of consumption and entitlement when it comes to sexual gratification.

There are certainly other symptoms of this consuming mind-set. One that is rampant among pastors and goes virtually without censure is the use of food to medicate stress and pain. Again, this problem is complex but some pastors who would never abuse alcohol, drugs, or pornography, and would soundly condemn those who do, at the very same time suffer the consequences of gross obesity. This is an issue of integrity if the condition lingers because they will not seek the help required to stop the pattern of overeating and pursue the disciplines of physical health.

The sinful consuming of gifts can also happen when pastors misunderstand and misuse the authorities that attach to the pastoral office. There is indeed a pastoral authority that is part of life in the church of Jesus Christ. This authority carries with it a sort of power that is easily abused unless this power is daily surrendered to Christ. As stated several times previously, pastors are representatives of Christ in the community of faith. This is a profound and sacred duty that comes upon us when we make our vows of ordination. In many ways we carry and reflect the offices of Christ as prophet, priest, and shepherd-king. When we take responsibility for the spiritual health of a people in congregation, there comes upon us a mantle of spiritual authority that is awesome and fearful. Great spiritual care must be taken to ensure that this real spiritual authority never gets out of the proper bounds by coming into the manipulative hands of a pastor who is not attending to prayer and fasting. Gladly, we are not left without resources in navigating faithfully these potential ethical traps, and to these resources we now turn.[2]

Resources for Being True

There are several powerful resources available to pastors that, under the power of the Spirit, can become avenues for the development of strong character and unwavering integrity in the life of a pastor. Chief among these are the disciplines of spiritual formation that include, among many others, prayer, Bible reading, fasting, and solitude.

My counsel here is simply that pastors would give themselves faithfully to the exercise of these disciplines in a regular pattern. I know this is easier said than done in the face of never-ending demands on their time and energy. I do believe that pastors have generally been too isolated in this area, going it alone far too often in their practices of and accountability for spiritual formation. We need the fellowship of colleagues. Overseers in the church should turn much of their influence toward assisting pastors in accessing the available resources for spiritual growth and intentional discipleship.

A significant component of all of this is the discipline of keeping Sabbath. This was a focus in chapter 9, so in this context I would simply remind us that pastors tend to be chief among Sabbath breakers. I think this is because they are so good at justifying any number of activities as either "ox in the ditch" critical or as somehow part of Sabbath keeping simply because they fall on the Lord's Day. Could it be that many, if not most, of the ethical traps into which clergy fall, or the fractures of integrity in our lives, are rooted in a failure to cease from work for an entire day and trust God to provide? I am hearing the protests of my bivocational brothers and sisters even as I write that. I do not really know the answer to the weighty dilemma you face. However, I cannot minimize the fact that we simply to do not have authority to change God's plan that was weaved into the very fabric of creation: the rhythm of work and rest without which our lives collapse into exile.

For pastors who are married and live in nuclear families, the intentional nurture of these relationships can certainly become a huge resource for the nurture of our integrity. It has been mentioned in several contexts here that pastoral ministry places great stress on clergy marriages. Yet clergy couples can be among the most reticent of Christians to seek continuing education and counseling for their relationships, not to mention the possible need for intervention and therapy. Let me simply urge my colleagues to discover what Starla and I have found in our thirty-four years of marriage: there is great freedom and growth to be realized when we stop pretending that we have it all together and become unafraid to name what hurts. This honesty opens the way for us to receive the healing grace of God.

A tremendous resource in all of this is the discipline of physical health. This connects to the above conversation about gluttony, but it is also about more than overeating. Daily physical exercise is a powerful resource for dealing with the unusual stresses of pastoral ministry. If you have not yet embraced a discipline and regimen of physical exercise, start somewhere. Begin by taking a thirty-minute walk each day. Take the stairs rather than the elevator when you visit in the hospital. Do something that can begin to move you in the direction of greater physical health and the release of stress, which can be incredibly damaging.

Finally, the most important practical resource in my opinion for maintaining a life of integrity (recognizing grace as essential) is the power of accountability. Clearly, the foundational accountability is that which is offered by God. By grace we are invited to participate in the life-giving communion of our triune God. But we also have the gift of accountable relationships with one another. If we are married, our relationship with the spouse is a critical accountable relationship. No one knows us better, and no one is in any better position to see the potential compromises and pitfalls of keeping integrity between the public self and the private self. The best thing I ever heard my wife say about me is, "He is the same person at home as you see on Sunday." If my wife, children, and grandchildren can testify in this way, I have won a great spiritual victory. Additionally, all of us need the counsel of a close friend or two who will look at our lives in a more objective way than perhaps even family can do. I have enjoyed the privilege of sitting with my friend Dave Warner nearly every Friday morning for the past twenty years. Over coffee and bagels, we have shared our victories and our struggles and have prayed for each other that we might be found men who are true. All those years ago we borrowed a set of seven accountability questions from Charles Swindoll and have used them every week since.[3] I have no doubt that this weekly practice has been a huge factor in helping to keep me true and faithful to all of my vows, including my ordination vows.

The 1993 film *Shadowlands* is about the life of C. S. Lewis, including his later-in-life marriage to Joy Gresham. One of the compelling and convicting moments of the story is when Lewis blesses his dying wife with the words, "You are the truest person I have ever known." When my life's journey is ended, I pray that those closest to me would be able, at least in some degree, to attach this beautiful epitaph to me. When I am finally with the Lord, awaiting the resurrection, I hope my children and grandchildren discover the certificate of my ordination. And when they do, I pray that its discovery will bring nothing but satisfaction and joy as they celebrate a life that was true.

Part 3

FAITHFUL AND EFFECTIVE: RIGHTLY ASSESSING PASTORAL WORK

17
SUCCESS

The idea of success should be simple because success is generally defined as achieving our aim or accomplishing our purpose. It may seem that this would be easily assessed. Either we accomplished the goal or we did not. If my goal is to write a book, I can mark success by completion of the manuscript or perhaps by the acceptance of it by a publisher. But there is a whole other arena of evaluation on which we often seem to base our sense of success. Will anyone *like* my book? Will the people who read it think it is helpful, encouraging, or perhaps even important? When the idea of success begins to be judged on these more subjective criteria, our sense of accomplishment may be a bit more intangible.

Perhaps this is why the idea of success is an ever-elusive category for pastors. Regardless of how impressive the metrics of our ministry may be (size of congregation, number of people baptized, etc.), we all know that the measures that really matter most to us are more difficult to quantify. In fact, they probably cannot be quantified at all. So how should we think about success for the purpose of evaluating our ministries? Surely, we would turn first to Scripture—but where to look? We could certainly look to the stories of individuals God used in powerful ways among his people. Abraham, Joseph, Moses, Joshua, Gideon, Saul, David, Solomon—it doesn't take long to realize that these stories are filled with failure and success, which is just the nature of life in this world, isn't it? Maybe rather than identifying success with any particular example (other than Jesus, of course), it would be helpful to think about it from the standpoint of grace. What does the inviting, including, searching, and pursuing reach of God to us say about how we ought to think about whether or not we have been successful in fulfilling God's call?

Concerning this, I hear the words of Paul to the Ephesians, "For we are God's handiwork, created in Christ Jesus to do good works, which God prepared in advance for us to do" (2:10). The way that this challenges me in my thinking about success is in the realization that too often I have sought to define my success on the basis of the works that I set out to do. If, however, my life's work really has been "prepared in advance" for me by God, then my measure of success is no longer the achievement of my goals but the fulfillment of God's purposes for me. In this regard I think of the New Testament word *teleios*, usually translated as "mature" or "perfect." Paul uses a form of the word (*teleion*) in the Ephesian letter, writing, "until we all reach unity in the faith and in the knowledge of the Son of God and become *mature*, attaining to the whole measure of the fullness of Christ" (4:13, emphasis added). It is a beautiful word that carries the ideas of consummation and completion. Thinking of the individual's response to grace and relationship to God, it is about fulfilling our God-given purpose not of our own ability or volition but wholly on the basis of God's grace. It is, in fact, being faithful.

There are voices that resist defining success for pastors on the basis of being faithful. The argument seems to go that just being faithful is not enough, that somehow one could be faithful while also being completely ineffective, as if faithfulness is just sticking it out to the end. It seems to me that the idea of effectiveness is so imbedded in what it means to be faithful that the one cannot be conceived without the other. What does it mean for me to be faithful to my marriage vows? If it only means that I stick it out to the bitter end, then I am quite sure I have missed the point of faithfulness. My success in ministry is about more than just making it to the end, and it is certainly about more than any manner of impressive statistics that might be noted. Success is *teleion*, fulfilling the purpose for which God created us and to which God called us. It is faithfulness to our call that demands our best in every assignment.

But what should I do when my best does not look as good as my colleague's best? Perhaps one reason that embracing the idea of success is difficult for pastors is because there is a real competitive streak in us. It is commonly known that when pastors get together, sooner or later the conversation will get around to the question, "So what are you running now?" The question is not about the path I take for my morning jog; it is about the average weekly attendance at my church. We love to say that this doesn't really matter, but the pastors who get invited to speak for the conferences, hold the seminars, and write the books are generally the pastors who have been "successful" as defined by the growth (numeric or popular) of the organization. I hope that we are moving past this kind of thinking, and we are finding help from an emerging generation of pastors who do not seem to be so impressed by the lure of leading a large church or being "promoted" in the ecclesial hierarchy. There does seem to be a growing recognition that "bigger" is not necessarily "better" and that the work of the kingdom of God, instead of being front and center, regularly moves to the margins.

Reward (financial or otherwise) and recognition will probably always be a part of how human beings organize society and assign place and value. Pastors can be tempted to use these measures of success and consequently allow pride, fear, and envy to harm the experience of authentic community among the corps of pastors. The best way I know to keep this from happening is for all of us to take the posture of life and ministry that was embraced by our Lord. I submit that this is the biblical definition of success:

> *[Christ Jesus], being in very nature God,*
> *did not consider equality with God something*
> *to be used to his own advantage;*
> *rather, he made himself nothing*
> *by taking the very nature of a servant,*
> *being made in human likeness.*
> *And being found in appearance as a man,*
> *he humbled himself*
> *by becoming obedient to death—*
> *even death on a cross!*

Therefore God exalted him to the highest place
and gave him the name that is above every name,
that at the name of Jesus every knee should bow,
in heaven and on earth and under the earth,
and every tongue acknowledge that Jesus Christ is Lord,
to the glory of God the Father. (Phil. 2:6-11)

18
LEGACY

Just one brief note more on something that is at the core of what it means to be successful in ministry: legacy. I am not using this word in its usual definition as it applies to the money, property, or reputations we leave behind for later generations. The kind of legacy I am thinking about is the purposeful investment we make in those who come after us in vocational ministry. There are two key ways that pastors do this work.

The first is by nurturing the call of God in the lives of others. As was noted in chapter 3, God's calling of particular Christians into the life of service through pastoral work most often emerges within the context of a congregation. The work of the Spirit in calling men and women to the pastorate is not an individualistic affair. The wooing of the Spirit is personal, but it is also always communal. I remember here again how God's call to me came into focus largely through my community of faith and especially through my pastor, who helped me make sense of the "still small voice" of God (1 Kings 19:12, KJV). Rev. Wallace somehow saw it as part of his pastoral responsibility to fan into the flame this pilot-light work of the Spirit in the life of a young teenager whose future was uncertain. For all of the time that my pastor invested in me, there was no guarantee and maybe not even a real confident hope that there would be any significant return on the investment. For Pastor Wallace it was simply the right thing to do as one who understood that the calling that had been given to him included the mission to develop future pastors. I was not the only person who benefited from his ministry in this regard, for throughout his nearly fifty-year ministry he gave himself to this work. I am regularly aware of the gratitude I have for this gift that was given to me at a critical time in my life.

Sometimes our work in nurturing the call of others will be clear and specific, as in my personal story. I think there are many other times when our influence in these ways is not quite as evident but no less significant. I believe that only eternity will fully reveal the myriad of ways in which our lives have been influential in the calling and shaping of other pastors. The result is not for us to manage, only that we think about this component of our work with prayerful intention. When God is calling young people into vocational ministry, is it not reasonable to assume that God would also speak to their pastors about it? I do think that part of the work of the Spirit in us could include the clear sense that God is at work in the life of young persons under our influence, drawing them into pastoral work. We need to pay attention to these promptings and act upon them.

In considering these young persons, it is probably not wise to say, "God told me that you are to be a pastor." What we should do is begin praying for them about the possibility of God's call. It is our duty as pastors to cover them with our prayers, asking God to work in their lives by bringing not only clarity but also release from the initial fear that can so easily come when God calls one's name. Then we need to look for opportunities to engage them in conversations about their dreams and plans. There may come a point in these conversations, when trust has been developed as well as a sense of authentic friendship, that we should name the possibility that God could be calling them to a life of service as pastors, as missionaries, or in other roles of ordained ministry. This is likely not a "God told me" word but more of a "have you ever thought about" conversation. It is casting vision, nurturing dreams, raising possibilities, and calling our young friends to account for obedience to whatever becomes the direction of the Spirit in their lives.

Recently I was part of a service where the speaker was a colleague who serves as a missionary. The sanctuary was packed with hundreds of teenagers as well as adults. The missionary gave his testimony of what it was like for him as a young man to surrender to the call of God in his life. He went to college on an impressive football scholarship and was chasing the dream shared by many young men of playing professional football. His story was about God's relentless call to give his life in vocational ministry. It was a simple yet compelling story that ended with the missionary casting a pointed and clear question to his hearers. Would they be willing to recognize that God may be calling some of them in similar ways? Would they commit to obedient response to whatever God desires for their lives? We have heard those kinds of appeals many times, but it reminded me again that nurturing the call of God in the lives of others is a central and critical work for every pastor.

Another significant way in which we attend to this legacy of vocational ministry is through the work of mentoring. During a recent sabbatical, part of my learning was to realize that I have too often assumed that every young pastor received what I was blessed to receive through several outstanding mentors. The fact is, this simply is not the case. Added to this is the increase I am experiencing (probably because I am now a grandfather) of younger pastors seeking a mentoring conversation with me. I give high priority to these requests for my time, and I am realizing in these conversations that perhaps the majority of developing ministers have not received the kind of mentoring that I had.

Further prompting my awareness of this issue was my encounter with the recent work of Gordon MacDonald through both his book *Going Deep: Becoming a Person of Influence*[1] and through a half-day of sitting under his teaching. His focus is on a simple but life-altering question: "What is required to produce leaders who can serve for a period of fifty years and grow deeper, stronger, wiser, and more effective with each decade of life?" MacDonald describes how he and his wife are giving themselves in new ways in their autumn years to spending more time with fewer people. Their attention is centered on intentionally selecting people they discern to have capacity for going deep spiritually and in ministry. This does not necessarily mean that the people they select are the most talented or would be judged by others as having the greatest promise. They are people who are open and hungry to know God and to be faithful to the call of God on their lives. It is about investing in people for the long haul, with the long-range view in mind.

For the rest of my days I want to invest in a legacy of faithfulness. I can help foster that kind of legacy through the intentional ministry of mentoring those who are coming behind me. And I call upon my pastoral colleagues who are men and women "of a certain age"—those of us with enough history to have some perspective and with enough spiritual growth (by the grace of God) to have some wisdom—to join me in pursuing mentoring relationships with developing ministers. On a few occasions, I have had younger colleagues seek me out and ask me to mentor them. This is great and sets a strong foundation for the relationship. But I also need to look around for those who may not take that initiative for any number of reasons. It would be a mistake to judge the lack of initiative in this regard as lack of interest or po-tential. Probably half of our best pastors are introverted in personality and just would not reach out in this way, so we need to do it. And the rewards are great. Investing in our young friends can bring fresh perspective to a weary soul.

EPILOGUE

One final word to acknowledge what is no doubt obvious. The life and work of pastoral ministry is vast and complex. There are so many components to this calling and so many nuances of all that I have tried to discuss in this book. I am aware that I have left many important issues for other books and other conversations. This is actually one of the main reasons I attempted this work—from the belief that more of us need to add our experiences to the body of knowledge and wisdom that has been collected so far on this amazing life of pastoral ministry. I do not imagine that this simple offering is in any way definitive of the pastoral office. Where I have erred in fact or in your judgment, I beg your forgiveness and invite your correction. Where I have contributed something helpful, I thank the Lord.

And now, to him who is able to keep you from stumbling and to present you before his glorious presence without fault and with great joy—to the only God our Savior be glory, majesty, power and authority, through Jesus Christ our Lord, before all ages, now and forevermore! Amen.
—Jude vv. 24-25

ACKNOWLEDGMENTS

First, thanks to my friend Bonnie Perry of Beacon Hill Press of Kansas City. Bonnie not only encouraged this work from her professional context but also models respect for the pastoral office and support of pastors in her local congregation. Bonnie, your belief in me is a gift of grace for which I am deeply thankful.

The initial development of this project came into being during a nine-week sabbatical from my duties as superintendent of the Kansas City District of the Church of the Nazarene. Thanks to the District Advisory Board for supporting the gift of sabbatical. Special thanks to the team I work with each day that "held down the fort" so capably while I was away, especially my wife, Starla. Thanks also to the pastors of the Kansas City District who are my friends and colleagues in ministry. Several of them offered key suggestions for this work. My gratitude goes particularly to Rusty Brian, Keith Davenport, Joe Foltz, and Stephanie Lobdell for reading the manuscript along the way and offering helpful comments.

I began to list the names of my elders in ministry who have had a profound and shaping influence on me throughout my ministerial development. I realized that it was simply not possible to make an accurate list, having been so abundantly blessed with brothers and sisters in the pastoral office from whom I have learned so much and have been greatly encouraged. However, two mentors deserve special mention: Rev. Edward W. Wallace and Dr. Richard L. Young. I will forever be indebted to these dear brothers who have loved me like a son, as I have loved each of them like a father. Thank you for the gift of your investment in me.

NOTES

Introduction

1. Andrew Purves, *Pastoral Theology in the Classical Tradition* (Louisville, KY: Westminster John Knox, 2001), 122.

2. My abiding gratitude to Rev. Edward and Marjorie Wallace for their godly example.

3. Reference is to 1 Chronicles 12:32.

4. Gordon Lathrop, *The Pastor, a Spirituality* (Minneapolis: Fortress Press, 2006), 18.

5. Howard Snyder, *Yes in Christ! Wesleyan Reflections on Gospel, Mission, and Culture* (Toronto: Clements Academic, 2011), 72.

Chapter 1

1. John Wesley, Preface to *Sermons on Several Occasions*, in *The Works of John Wesley* (Kansas City: Beacon Hill Press of Kansas City, 1978), 5:3.

2. Thomas Oden, *John Wesley's Teachings*, vol. 1 (Grand Rapids: Zondervan, 2012), 66.

3. I am aware of more recent conversations regarding the so-called quadrilateral, which serve as helpful corrections to ways in which this idea is sometimes used. An excellent summary of these conversations can be found in T. A. Noble, *Holy Trinity: Holy People: The Theology of Christian Perfecting* (Eugene, OR: Cascade Books, 2013).

4. "Argument" in this sense means rational sequencing more than debate.

5. For example, letter to the Rev. Dr. Conyers Middleton (January 4, 1749). Of course, Wesley draws this from Article IV of the Church of England's Thirty-Nine Articles.

6. Church of the Nazarene, *2009-2013 Manual Church of the Nazarene*, Article IV, The Holy Scriptures (Kansas City: Nazarene Publishing House, 2009).

7. See N. T. Wright, *Scripture and the Authority of God* (New York: HarperCollins, 2005), for an accessible conversation on this point.

8. Note the excellent volume edited by Barry Callen and Richard Thompson, *Reading the Bible in Wesleyan Ways* (Kansas City: Beacon Hill Press of Kansas City, 2004).

9. As we will discuss later, this contrasts with many modern models of pastoral life and work that seem to find their bases more in organizational leadership or business principles than in the first principles of a relational God (i.e., self-sacrificing love).

10. Eugene Peterson, *Five Smooth Stones for Pastoral Work* (Grand Rapids: Eerdmans, 1980).

11. Thomas Oden, *Classical Pastoral Care*, 4 vols. (Grand Rapids: Baker Publishing, 1987).

12. Purves, *Pastoral Theology*.

Chapter 2

1. Wesley, "An Address to the Clergy," in *Works of John Wesley*, 10:484.

2. Purves, *Pastoral Theology*, 2.

3. Lathrop, *The Pastor, a Spirituality*, 17.

4. Stephen R. Covey, *The 7 Habits of Highly Effective People* (New York: Free Press, 1987), 287.

Chapter 3

1. George MacDonald, *The Curate's Awakening* (Grand Rapids: Bethany House, 1993), 176.

2. William Willimon, *Calling and Character: Virtues of the Ordained Life* (Nashville: Abingdon Press, 2000), 44.

Chapter 4

1. Joseph Ratzinger, *Jesus of Nazareth: From the Baptism in the Jordan to the Transfiguration* (New York: Doubleday, 2007), 130.

2. Eugene Peterson, *Practice Resurrection: A Conversation on Growing Up in Christ* (Grand Rapids: Eerdmans, 2010), 70.

3. John Wesley, *A Plain Account of Christian Perfection* (Kansas City: Beacon Hill Press of Kansas City, 1966), 109.

4. Lathrop, *The Pastor, a Spirituality*, 18.

5. Ibid., viii. He is actually quoting here from George Herbert's *Country Parson*.

6. Charles Wesley, "Come, Let Us Use the Grace Divine," in *Wesley Hymns* (Kansas City: Lillenas Publishing, 1982), 109.

7. E. Dee Freeborn, *When You Pray: Going Everywhere with Jesus* (Kansas City: Beacon Hill Press of Kansas City, 1992).

Chapter 5

1. Donald McGavran, *Understanding Church Growth*, 3rd ed. (Grand Rapids: Eerdmans, 1980), xiv.

2. Eugene Peterson, *Working the Angles: The Shape of Pastoral Integrity* (Grand Rapids: Eerdmans, 1987), 2.

Chapter 6

1. Richard B. Ryding, "The Identification of Occupational Stressors that Precipitate Burnout among Clergy in the Church of the Nazarene," M.A. thesis (Wheaton, IL: Wheaton College, 1984).

2. *2009-2013 Manual*, 189.

3. I first got this term from Marva Dawn.

4. Peterson, *Working the Angles*.

5. Ibid., 45.

6. The works of Thomas Merton and of Walter Brueggemann are two examples of this.

7. Peterson, *Working the Angles*, 154.

8. Ibid., 162.

9. Mary Rose O'Reilly, "Deep Listening: An Experimental Friendship," *Weavings*, vol. IX, no. 3 (May/June 1994): 19.

Chapter 7

1. Henri Nouwen, *The Road to Daybreak: A Spiritual Journey* (New York: Doubleday, 1988), 98.

2. Thomas à Kempis, *The Imitation of Christ* (Uhrichsville, OH: Barbour and Co., 1984), bk. 3, chap. 23, no. 3.

3. *2009-2013 Manual*, para. 417.

4. Note the fine book on this subject by Timothy Gaines and Shawna Songer Gaines, *A Seat at the Table: A Generation Reimagining Its Place in the Church* (Kansas City: Beacon Hill Press of Kansas City, 2012).

5. John Wesley, "On Schism." As quoted by Thomas Oden, *John Wesley's Teachings*, vol. 3, *Pastoral Theology* (Grand Rapids: Zondervan, 2012), 232.

6. Ibid., 234.

Chapter 8

1. *2009-2013 Manual*, 181.

2. Ibid., 247.

3. Purves, *Pastoral Theology*, 18.

4. *2009-2013 Manual*, 247.

Chapter 9

1. Thomas Oden, *Ancient Christian Commentary on Scripture*, 29 vols. (Downers Grove, IL: InterVarsity Press, 2001).

Chapter 10

1. Henri Nouwen, *Making All Things New: An Invitation to the Spiritual Life* (San Francisco: HarperCollins, 1981), 24.

2. Peterson, *Working the Angles*, 4.

3. Dan Spaite, *Time Bomb in the Church: Defusing Pastoral Burnout* (Kansas City: Beacon Hill Press of Kansas City, 1999).

Chapter 11

1. I am referring here to the work of *Preacher's Magazine,* which I co-edited with David Busic from 1999 to 2007.

2. Lathrop, *The Pastor,* 41.

3. Billy Graham et al., *The Pastor's Guide to Effective Preaching* (Kansas City: Beacon Hill Press of Kansas City, 2003).

4. *The Revised Common Lectionary* is located at http://lectionary.library.vander bilt.edu.

Chapter 12

1. John Telford, *The Life of John Wesley,* chap. 14. Retrieved from http://wesley.nnu .edu/john-wesley/the-life-of-john-wesley-by-john-telford/the-life-of-john-wesley -by-john-telford-chapter-14.

2. Tom Noble, *Holy Trinity: Holy People: The Theology of Christian Perfecting* (Eugene, OR: Cascade Books, 2013), 35.

3. From the Ritual for Sacrament of the Lord's Supper, *2009-2013 Manual,* 252.

Chapter 13

1. *2009-2013 Manual,* para. 401.2.

2. Ibid.

3. John Wesley, *The Use of Money,* Sermon 50. Retrieved from http://wesley .nnu.edu/john-wesley/the-sermons-of-john-wesley-1872-edition/sermon-50-the -use-of-money/.

Chapter 14

1. Justin Martyr, *Apology,* chap. 67. Retrieved from http://earlychristianwritings .com/text/justinmartyr-firstapology.html.

2. See Robert Webber's works for a thorough study of the fourfold pattern of worship.

3. An excellent lectionary is located at http://lectionary.library.vanderbilt.edu.

4. John Wesley, *Twenty-Five Articles of Religion, Article 17.* Retrieved from http:// www.imarc.cc/br/br2/wesley25ar17.htm.

5. *Sing to the Lord* hymnal, no. 739 (Kansas City: Lillenas Publishing, 1993).

6. From the Book of Common Prayer. Retrieved from http://www.bcponline .org.

7. *2009-2013 Manual,* 252.

8. From the Book of Common Prayer.

9. This version from *The United Methodist Hymnal* (Nashville: United Method- ist Publishing House, 1989).

10. *2009-2013 Manual,* 253.

11. This is the name for a cable network television show about weddings. It de- buted in 2004 on the WEtv network.

12. Retrieved from http://weddingindustrystatistics.com.

13. Thomas G. Long, *Accompany Them with Singing: The Christian Funeral* (Louisville, KY: Westminster John Knox, 2009), xv.

14. Before you write one more funeral sermon, make sure you have read N. T. Wright's *Surprised by Hope* (New York: HarperOne, 2008).

Chapter 16

1. Retrieved from http://www.gallup.com/poll/1654/honesty-ethics-professions .aspx.

2. Note the excellent document from the National Association of Evangelicals titled *Code of Ethics for Pastors.* Located at http://www.nae.net/codeofethics.

3. A good list of accountability questions, including those from Swindoll, are located at http://www.christianitytoday.com/edstetzer/2008/may/accountability -questions.html.

Chapter 18

1. Nashville: Thomas Nelson Publishers, 2011.

SELECTED BIBLIOGRAPHY

Lathrop, Gordon. *The Pastor: A Spirituality*. Minneapolis: Fortress Press, 2006.

Long, Thomas. *Accompany Them with Singing: The Christian Funeral*. Louisville, KY: Westminster John Knox, 2009.

Maddix, Mark. *Pastoral Practices: A Wesleyan Paradigm*. Kansas City: Beacon Hill Press of Kansas City, 2013.

Maddox, Randy. *Responsible Grace: John Wesley's Practical Theology*. Nashville: Abingdon Press, 1994.

Oden, Thomas. *Classical Pastoral Care*. 4 vols. Grand Rapids: Baker Books, 1994.

_____. *John Wesley's Teachings*. 3 vols. Grand Rapids: Zondervan, 2012.

Petersen, Bruce. *Foundations of Pastoral Care*. Kansas City: Beacon Hill Press of Kansas City, 2006.

Peterson, Eugene. *The Contemplative Pastor: Returning to the Art of Spiritual Direction*. Grand Rapids: Eerdmans, 1993.

_____. *Five Smooth Stones for Pastoral Work*. Grand Rapids: Eerdmans, 1980.

_____. *The Pastor: A Memoir*. New York: Harper Collins, 2011.

_____. *Practice Resurrection: A Conversation on Growing Up in Christ*. Grand Rapids: Eerdmans, 2010.

_____. *Working the Angles: The Shape of Pastoral Integrity*. Grand Rapids: Eerdmans, 1994.

Purves, Andrew. *Pastoral Theology in the Classical Tradition*. Louisville, KY: Westminster John Knox, 2001.

Rowell, Jeren. *What's a Pastor to Do?: The Good and Difficult Work of Pastoral Ministry*. Kansas City: Beacon Hill Press of Kansas City, 2004.

Snyder, Howard. *Yes in Christ: Wesleyan Reflections on Gospel, Mission, and Culture*. Toronto: Clements Academic, 2011.

Willimon, William. *Calling and Character: Virtues of the Ordained Life*. Nashville: Abingdon Press, 2000.

_____. *Pastor: The Theology and Practice of Ordained Ministry*. Nashville: Abingdon Press, 2002.

Wright, N. T. *Surprised by Hope: Rethinking Heaven, the Resurrection, and the Mission of the Church*. New York: HarperOne, 2008.

Also by Jeren Rowell

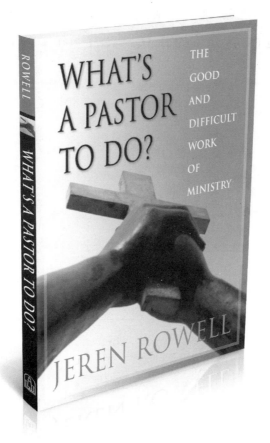

The work of a minister is mixed with the joy of serving the Savior and the frustration of leading people.

In *What's a Pastor to Do?* Dr. Jeren Rowell gives wisdom and encouragement to ministers in need of spiritual refreshment and comfort.

With short chapters that offer biblical insight, Scripture, and uplifting illustrations, this book is the perfect restorative tool for every minister who has asked, "What am I to do?"

What's a Pastor to Do?
By Jeren Rowell
ISBN: 978-0-8341-2207-9

BEACON HILL PRESS
OF KANSAS CITY

Available online at BeaconHillBooks.com

WESLEYAN PARADIGM SERIES

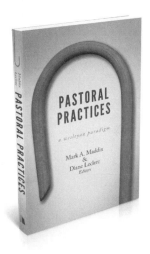

Pastoral Practices

Whatever the task may be—preaching, discipling, evangelizing, or administrating—this book sheds light on the way Wesleyan theology refines, informs, and enhances the theories and methods of each pastoral practice.

Pastoral Practices
Mark A. Maddix, Diane Leclerc (Editors)
978-0-8341-3009-8

Essential Church

Contributing pastors and educators explore the meaning, purpose, and function of the church as well as its structure. They address topics such as the kingdom of God, worship, and mission in relation to the body of Christ, and give special attention to Wesleyan theological concerns.

Essential Church
Diane Leclerc, Mark A. Maddix (Editors)
978-0-8341-3242-9

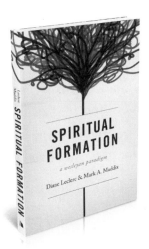

Spiritual Formation

People have a deep hunger and thirst for something that transcends them. This book focuses on how people can grow in Christlikeness while also providing guidance on self-care, spiritual direction, and mentoring.

Spiritual Formation
Diane Leclerc, Mark A. Maddix (Editors)
978-0-8341-2613-8

Also available in ebook formats

BEACON HILL PRESS
OF KANSAS CITY

Available online at BeaconHillBooks.com